DELETED

Poet-Critics AND THE
Administration OF Culture

Poet-Critics AND THE
Administration OF Culture

~~~~~~~~~~~~~~~~~~~~~~

EVAN KINDLEY

Harvard University Press

Cambridge, Massachusetts
London, England
2017

First printing

Library of Congress Cataloging-in-Publication Data

Names: Kindley, Evan, author.
Title: Poet-critics and the administration of culture / Evan Kindley.
Description: Cambridge, Massachusetts : Harvard University Press,
    2017. | Includes bibliographical references and index.
Identifiers: LCCN 2017008711 | ISBN 9780674980075 (alk. paper)
Subjects: LCSH: Authors and patrons—United States—History. |
    Critics—United States—History. | Modernism (Literature)—United
    States. | Litterateurs—United States—History. | United States—
    Intellectual life—20th century.
Classification: LCC E169.1 .K497 2017 | DDC 306.4/209730904—
    dc23 LC record available at https://lccn.loc.gov/2017008711

For my parents

Contents

Poet-Critics AND THE
Administration OF Culture

Introduction: Village Explainers

"HE WAS A VILLAGE explainer, excellent if you were a village, but if you were not, not," Gertrude Stein writes of Ezra Pound in *The Autobiography of Alice B. Toklas*.[1] Stein's joke at Pound's expense is justly famous. It is, among other things, an ingenious bit of avant-garde one-upmanship: Stein, perhaps the most mysterious and inscrutable of literary modernists, is insinuating that Pound's penchant for "explaining" his work and the work of his peers to the public made him less of an artist than, for example, Stein herself. The remark implies that explanation is yeoman's work, something necessary but unpleasant, and beneath the dignity of the artist. (As if explanation weren't bad enough, there's the provincial ring of the phrase: one should remember that the word "bourgeois" derives from the French word for "village.") Artists themselves, Stein suggests, have little need of critical explanation, especially when it is directed toward a "general," nonpoetic audience. At best, it may serve a didactic, democratizing function, helping initiate the philistine public into the mysteries of art and clarify avant-garde practice for "villagers" who might otherwise misunderstand or distrust it. At worst, it cheapens art by attempting to explain it away or cedes too much to social norms by trying to make difficult, experimental work palatable.

Stein, of course, did her fair share of self-explanation and self-popularization—*The Autobiography of Alice B. Toklas* is itself a work in this mold, albeit a cleverly ventriloquized one—but that is immaterial here. The attitude she adopts toward Pound's "village

1

explainer" role is one that is commonly, and not incorrectly, associated with modernism: mandarin, aloof, and automatically dismissive of vulgar oversimplification and the heresy of paraphrase. "Genuine poetry can communicate before it is understood," T. S. Eliot wrote in his 1929 essay on Dante, and similar formulas attesting to a preference for the fact of art over its elucidation have been asserted by virtually every writer one could call "modernist": "The poem is the poem, not its paraphrase" (Wallace Stevens); "No ideas but in things" (William Carlos Williams); "A poem should not mean / But be" (Archibald MacLeish).[2] Modernist difficulty by nature resists understanding and explanation; it prefers simple aesthetic facticity— "being"—to the elucidation of cognitive meaning or, to adapt the title of one of Stein's essays, "composition as explanation" to explanation per se.

Yet there is a paradox here insofar as most of the major modernists—not only Pound and Eliot but also Marianne Moore, Virginia Woolf, Williams, Stevens, Langston Hughes, André Breton, and even, in certain moods, Stein herself—were passionate explainers. Criticism, for the modernists, was a crucial way of publicizing their work, refining their aesthetics, and interacting with their contemporaries, and hardly any modernist managed to avoid leaving behind a sizable corpus of literary criticism. Moreover, it is largely thanks to the developments of the modernist period that we now expect poets—and, more and more, other types of creative artists as well— to explain their work to us as well as to produce it. Indeed, this activity of self-explanation forms part of the "routine autopoiesis" that Mark McGurl sees as essential to modernism. "In the modernist tradition, the portrait of the artist is not only an important single book and an important genre, but also a name for one of the routine operations of literary modernism. For the modernist artist, that is, the reflexive production of the 'modernist artist'—i.e., job description itself—is a large part of the job."[3] In much the same spirit, we might say that the reflexive production of explanations, analyses, and critiques of modernist writing forms an essential part of the overall modernist project. Despite modernism's theoretical commitment to authorial impersonality and formal autonomy, imagining the great works of twentieth-century literature without their authorized paratexts—manifestos, personal statements, exegeses, footnotes, and justifications—is next to impossible. There is no modernism without its village explainers.

It was, at one time, a striking fact that many of the most prominent and respected poets of the early twentieth century were also prolific literary and cultural critics. If this phenomenon seems relatively mundane today, we can fairly describe this as one of modernism's legacies. Modernists were not the first poet-critics, but they were the first to establish a particular archetype that still pertains nearly a hundred years later, a job description that those who desire a career in poetry still have to fit. In the early twenty-first century we have grown accustomed to the idea of the poet as critic; indeed, it is one of the things we tend to expect any serious professional poet to be. (The other is a teacher.) Poets write closely argued essays for little magazines like *Boston Review*, *n+1*, and *Guernica* and book reviews for major media outlets like the *New York Times* and the *New York Review of Books*. Poets teach courses in critical theory to graduate students and publish abstract philosophical statements of poetics alongside their new creative work. Poets organize conferences whose participants and audiences are other poets. And poets are, increasingly, not just the foremost experts on poetry in our culture but the only experts.

Although the term "poet-critic" appears to have gained currency only in the mid-twentieth century, the combination of poetic and critical prose writing into a single vocation is by no means a modernist invention.[4] There is a long and august tradition of poets who have written critical prose on literary and cultural subjects, including Philip Sidney, John Dryden, John Milton, Samuel Johnson, Samuel Taylor Coleridge, Percy Bysshe Shelley, Ralph Waldo Emerson, and Matthew Arnold, to list only the most obvious and prestigious Anglo-American names. All the modernist poet-critics discussed in this book were aware of this tradition and in many cases actively invoked and revised it.

Moreover, although there are certainly doctrinal similarities among the poet-critics of the modernist period that distinguish them from their predecessors and successors, one should not insist too strongly—or, at least, I will not be insisting here—on the novelty of the particular critical theories espoused by the modernists. For decades, modernism's anxious insistence on its radical newness has misled many scholars into overemphasizing the degree of its discontinuity from literary history in one direction or another, whether through its purported destruction of a Romantic ideology or the postmodern deconstruction of modernism's ideological assumptions.

But the durable association between poet-critics and modernism is not merely a function of historical amnesia. Modernist poet-critics did play a distinctive part in literary history, one that still affects us today, and there are good reasons to distinguish the modernist poet-critic from the poet-critic in general. My object in this book is not ideological or aesthetic but institutional: I am less interested in the theories and the values that modernist critics promoted than in the opportunities they seized for promoting them and the compromises they made in order to do so. To make my case, I chronicle a tumultuous period that began in the late 1910s, when Eliot started to publish the insurrectionary and widely influential essays collected in *The Sacred Wood*, and ended in the late 1940s, when poet-critics, with the support of large bureaucratic institutions like research universities, government agencies, and philanthropic foundations, began to consolidate modernism's gains by making a durable place for it in the postwar American social order. The importance of this era is not that it produced a new kind of literary figure—"the poet-critic"—but that it found a new kind of work for this figure to perform. What is exceptional about the modernist poet-critics I discuss is not the fact that they wrote criticism, nor is it the particular type of criticism they wrote. It is that they participated, as none of their predecessors had or could have, in the life of bureaucracy, aligning themselves with large institutions at a time of radical instability in the cultural economy. They were not just poet-critics; they were poet-administrators.

୬ଡ଼ ୬ଡ଼ ୬ଡ଼

The modernist turn to bureaucratic administration was born of necessity. The old model of private patronage that had sustained modernism in its early decades was in crisis. The 1920s were the last decade in which elite literary production was supported primarily by wealthy patrons like Scofield Thayer, Lady Rothermere, Arthur Springarn, Carl Van Vechten, and John Quinn. This funding model was a casualty of the Great Depression and World War II, which together immiserated the patron class and shifted the priorities of many capitalists from Medici-style beneficence to simple self-preservation. The combination of two world wars and the market crash of 1929, as Thomas Piketty has argued, initiated a "euthanasia of the rentier" (a phrase borrowed from John Maynard Keynes).[5] The capital reserves of the class that had supported the experiments of modernism and the avant-garde in the early years of the century were seriously depleted, or sometimes wiped out entirely, by these shocks.

In place of the vanished aristocratic patrons came a set of interlinked bureaucratic institutions: the federal government, philanthropic foundations, and universities. All three served a similar role of protecting modernism and modernists from an unregulated free market that was assumed to be uninterested in, if not actively hostile to, the survival of the arts, and in particular poetry—the least remunerative and, in the popular imagination anyway, least materialist of art forms. Fears about the incompatibility of poetry with the free market antedate the rise of modernism, of course. Around the turn of the twentieth century, as John Timberman Newcomb demonstrated in *Would Poetry Disappear?*, an anxious social Darwinist discourse about this topic, positing the inevitable extinction of poetry in the modern era, began to appear in the pages of magazines like *Forum*, *Lippincott's*, and the *Dial*. According to Newcomb, "Poetry's crisis of value erupted in this gap between its desertion by mainstream cultural economies and the invention of alternative modern forms of publication—above all, the little magazine."[6]

But while Newcomb is committed to a narrative of cultural reconciliation, in which modernist poets found a way to reconnect with a popular audience through the medium of the little magazine, other scholars, like Lawrence Rainey, have tended to emphasize modernism's panicked flight from market capitalism in the 1910s and 1920s. "Modernism," Rainey writes, quoting Terry Eagleton's "Capitalism, Modernism, and Postmodernism," "is commonly considered 'a strategy whereby the work of art resists commodification, holds out by the skin of its teeth' against the loss of aesthetic autonomy. But it may be," he goes on, in good dialectical fashion, "that just the opposite would be a more accurate account: that modernism, among other things, is a strategy whereby the work of art invites and solicits its own commodification, but does so in such a way that it becomes a commodity of a special sort, one that is temporarily exempted from the exigencies of immediate consumption prevalent within the larger cultural economy, and instead is integrated into a different economic circuit of patronage, collecting, speculation, and investment." In Rainey's view, modernism is a sort of temporary holding action, "mark[ing] neither a straightforward resistance nor an outright capitulation to commodification but a momentary equivocation that incorporates elements of both in a brief, necessarily unstable synthesis."[7]

Like Rainey, I am concerned with the role of social institutions in shaping literary culture, and I find his account of how such institutions functioned during the heyday of high modernist patronage highly convincing. But I take him at his word when he suggests that modernism's speculative turn was, in broader historical terms, a "momentary equivocation" that rapidly and unexpectedly came to an end. What happened next? Rainey suggests that high modernism represented some kind of heroic last stand of aesthetic autonomy against the apocalyptic forces of commodification. What he does not say is that, in the postpatronage era, modernists—including, in some cases, those who had relied on wealthy patrons during the 1910s and 1920s—made new arrangements to support their work and protect it from the market, and that these arrangements involved not the largesse of wealthy private citizens but a variety of large bureaucratic institutions.

In positing a shift from an early phase in which modernist works circulated primarily as luxury commodities within networks of wealthy patrons to a postwar phase in which explanations and justifications of modernist practice circulated within bureaucratic institutions like universities and philanthropic foundations, I am extending Rainey's narrative about the alliance between modernism and the prestige/collector market. Although he does note in passing that "the Great Depression effectively eliminated the structures of private patronage that had sustained modernism's growth," his emphasis on speculative investment and the production of prestigious luxury commodities within a limited sphere of circulation fails to account for modernism's response to the worldwide crisis of capitalism precipitated by the stock market crash of 1929.[8] This was a crisis for poetry and its patrons, but also—as any moment of crisis tends to be—a major opportunity. The fact that so many poets, in the wake of Pound and Eliot, had styled themselves as poet-critics meant that they could now set themselves up as administrators and advisers at a time when such figures of authority and expertise were sorely needed to help legitimate the floundering enterprises of American capitalism and liberalism.

Poet-Critics and the Administration of Culture seeks to bridge the brief but significant historical gap between the cultural moment described by Rainey, in which modernism was largely sustained by elite individual patrons, and that described by scholars like Mc-Gurl, Eric Bennett, Greg Barnhisel, and Stephen Schryer, in which modernism becomes a matter of academic administration, government policy, and philanthropic concern.[9] I focus on the transitional period from 1920 to 1950, which saw, first, the slow reconstruction of the European economy after World War I, followed by the virtual obliteration of the world financial system as a result of the stock market crash of 1929, the rise of fascist ideology in Germany, Italy, and Japan and its spread via war and other mechanisms of imperialism, and finally World War II, which ultimately involved every nation and nearly every citizen for whom modernism ever mattered. I realize that this makes for a familiar litany; the claim that these events decisively influenced modernism is uncontroversial. Many previous studies have examined the role that individual modernists played in the war effort (on both sides), as well as their responses to the Great Depression and the New Deal. Although I touch on these issues, my focus is less on the sacrifices modernists made for their country than on the benefits they hoped to secure for themselves and their fellow practitioners thereby. These shocks, in other words, not only were incorporated into modernists' work as thematic material but also changed the sorts of justifications and explanations of that work that they offered to the public, and even the nature of the public they were addressing.

❧❧❧

The institution that has done the most to promote, support, and promulgate modernist explanation, of course, is academia. In recent years, more and more scholars have come to view "the research university [as] the major literary institution" of postwar America, as McGurl puts it in the preface to *The Program Era*. The first thing to note is that most of this work has dealt with fiction rather than poetry. McGurl focuses on creative-writing programs, which he argues helped codify and democratize the techniques of modernist fiction. But poets, at least at first, were more welcome in English departments than they were in creative-writing programs; indeed, they were welcome in English departments long before fiction writers were, and they still seem more at home there today. Why should this be so? One plausible answer is that poets possessed a different form of cultural capital than fiction writers, whose work was always at least potentially, or hypothetically, salable. No matter how many novelists may have in fact been impoverished or committed to producing work with little or no market value, the association between fiction and commercial success persisted. Poetry, on the other hand, was (as we have seen) regarded as antithetical to market capitalism and tended to wear its unmarketability as a badge of honor. Poets were thus both more motivated to align themselves with the university and other bureaucratic institutions than fiction writers (who, at least until the advent of the Program Era, were better off chasing the market) and a better fit among professors and other professionals who saw their work as properly separate from the indignity of profit seeking and open competition.

Whatever the reasons, there is no question that poets played a central role in the academy well before fiction writers did. The romance between modernist poet-critics and literature professors goes back at least to the early 1920s, when Eliot's *The Sacred Wood* attracted the notice and respect of I. A. Richards. By 1945, they had made it official: figures like John Crowe Ransom, Allen Tate,

R. P. Blackmur, and William Empson were eminences in the academic world as much as in the strictly literary world of the little magazines. The much-vaunted New Criticism was largely a matter of operationalizing the insights and ad hoc methods of brilliant minds like Ransom and Empson, a process that gradually came to require the input of fewer and fewer actual poet-critics. (A turning point was Stanley Edgar Hyman's *The Armed Vision: A Study in the Methods of Modern Literary Criticism*, published in 1947, which includes chapters on Eliot, Empson, Blackmur, and Yvor Winters, among others.) Meanwhile, however, literature departments continued to hire poet-critics, little magazines (often funded by universities) continued to publish them, and the prestige of the archetype grew, reaching its apogee in the 1950s and early 1960s. There was some resistance, on the part of poet-critics, to the incorporation of modernism and its discursive traditions into the universities, but for the most part they saw academicization as an opportunity, and seized it. In his groundbreaking 1993 monograph *Hart Crane and Allen Tate: Janus-Faced Modernism*, Langdon Hammer insists on the mutual benefit to both poetry and criticism that academic specialization offered: "Poetry was criticism's way into the university, a form of knowledge through which New Critics like Tate established their authority without advanced degrees, against the resistance of historical scholars. . . . This is true, but it could also be turned around, since criticism was *poetry*'s way into the university too. The hyphenated form poet-critic expressed an addition, a further development: it indicated a poet with the capacity not only to write poems but to reflect on them, to write about them, and to teach them."[10]

It is important, however, not to pass too quickly from the aristocratic phase of modernism described by Rainey to the academic phase of modernism described by Hammer and McGurl. In between lies a whole series of attempts to elaborate, explain, and justify the ways of modernism within a variety of institutional contexts, including the literary-journalistic field, the little magazine, the undergraduate college, government agencies like the Library of Congress and the Federal Writers' Project, and philanthropic foundations. In these years poet-critics were explainers in search of villages, nomads of a sort, and our awareness of where they finally came to settle should not obscure our knowledge of their itinerary.

❧ ❧ ❧

This is a book about justification: the justification of literature, and of the difficult, experimental, elitist, unrepentantly unmarketable literature called "modernism" in particular. Critics typically seek to justify not only specific works of art but art itself; they are tasked, in any society, with the generation of endless answers to the question "What is the point of art?" and, inevitably, the corollary: "And why should we pay for it?" Justification, then, is an intellectual exercise that is crucial to the continued survival of intellectual life. Without justifications, we have nothing to fall back on except received wisdom, which, in a society dominated, as ours is, by market relations, means the calculation of profit.

Of course, other coherent and intellectually satisfying justifications are possible beyond the market one. The most valuable theoretical account of justification I know is *On Justification: Economies of Worth*, published by the sociologist Luc Boltanski and the economist Laurent Thévenot in 1991. Their book proposes an ingenious and useful framework for understanding how social actors justify their opinions, behavior, and judgments. (I should note that Boltanski and Thévenot's use of the word "justification" is even more expansive than mine: in their work, it refers to cognitive metajudgments about every part of human society, not just art or criticism.) The authors posit the existence of six universal "economies of worth," by which they mean systems in which the value of human actions is assessed. (Their categories include civic, market, inspired, fame, industrial, and domestic; the specific properties of each of these discourses needn't concern us here.) Borrowing from the tradition of Plato's *Republic*, Augustine's *City of God*, and other canonical works of political philosophy, Boltanski and Thévenot metaphorically describe each order of justification as a separate "city": the civic city, the city of fame, the industrial city, the domestic city, and so on. Each city has its own laws, customs, and interdictions, and the language of one may make little sense, or have little persuasive force, in another.[11]

The metaphorical connection between Boltanski and Thévenot's theoretical "cities" and Stein's imaginary "villages," while coincidental, is too tempting not to pursue. The period I examine in this book is one in which poet-critics shifted from explaining themselves and their work to the inhabitants of one "village" (patrons) to doing so to the inhabitants of another (administrators). Each of these orders requires different things of its explainers: different modes of justification, criticism, and address. In the earlier period, aristocratic values justified support for modernism. Modernism's patrons understood it as the twentieth-century iteration of Matthew Arnold's "best that has been thought and said": while it might sometimes be held to have revolutionary or radical implications for society at large, its primary value lay simply in being better, or more advanced, than other literature. ("Avant-garde," with its dual implications of modishness and moral rectitude, is a key term here.) Poet-critics in this village made their appeals to elite patrons, wealthy people with "taste." The support that these patrons gave to artists was not presumed to be "good" in the ethical sense; it was simply an encouragement of what was "best" in the aesthetic sense. Nor was it the "best" according to the market; although the work of the artist was, for its aristocratic supporters, a kind of commodity, it was one that was precious precisely because only those with refined sensibilities could recognize its real value. The audience for this kind of work was never assumed to be very large (it often was as small as a single individual collector), and the rhetoric of smallness and sparseness was often exploited; the term "little magazine" is an example of this, as are the names of several of the most important and prominent little magazines of the modernist period: the *Little Review*, the *Smart Set*, *Coterie*, and others. Indeed, it was the little magazine (along with the undergraduate college, another institution structured by the values of exclusivity and smallness) that served as the central institution and paradigmatic organizational form during the high modernist period.

In the years after the 1929 crash, the population of this village began to decline. Poet-critics like Archibald MacLeish and Sterling Brown flocked first to the nation-state, arguing, somewhat counterintuitively, for modernism's role in preserving, protecting, and

improving democracy itself. There was much talk of ennobling the
spirit and enhancing liberty, as well as renewed attention to literature's propagandistic and inspirational functions. The audience for
this work was presumed to be large—in principle, universal, or at
least national. Two somewhat wishful and dubious notions underlay
this democratic rhetoric: first, that everyone in the nation personally benefited from the continued existence of modernist literature;
and second, that modernism might have an active role to play in the
defense of democracy against fascism (and, in some versions, communism). Support for literature and art was one more vital social
function that the rapidly expanding welfare state needed to under-
take. Modernism was conceived as a political project, but a nationalist one rather than one framed in opposition to the liberal state, as
it often had been by writers on both the left and the right in the
1910s and 1920s. It was, rather, a project that was fully compatible
with the aims of the U.S. government and was in fact impossible to
complete without it. The state was the only organizational form capable of transforming modernism from a niche interest of the idle
rich into a putatively progressive force within American culture.

By 1950, primarily technocratic values justified support for modernism. The size of this village expanded enormously in the years
after World War II, coming into being in tandem with the explo-
sion of the American research university and the rapid development
of the nonprofit philanthropic sector, and in important ways it is
still the dominant paradigm for writers and artists working in the
tradition of modernism today. This new technocratic village combined aspects of the aristocratic and the democratic into a new, slightly
improbable synthesis. As in the early years of high modernism,
elites—and aristocratic taste—were appealed to, and aesthetic values
were assumed to take precedence over ethical ones. But support for
advanced art was not accomplished through arbitrary charitable
handouts but was administered, as in the 1930s, via broad-based
bureaucratic institutions; and ethical justifications, though not
paramount, were still in circulation. There was no rhetoric of
aristocratic exclusivity—the number of beneficiaries could be, in
principle, as large as the number of people interested in literature—but neither was it assumed that everybody benefited; art was

not like Social Security. Modernist village explainers had a different case to make to technocrats than they did to aristocrats, with their mandarin zeal for excellence, or to democrats, with their utopian nationalist vision. In the technocratic postwar era, modernism was simply what top experts told us was our "greatest" literature—that was all. The real work was in selecting the experts. And poet-critics, I will try to show in what follows, represented some of these institutions' most valuable experts.

꿍ᇰ 꿍ᇰ 꿍ᇰ

My first two chapters concern poet-critics who operated squarely within the aristocratic framework, explaining and justifying modernism to a small minority of wealthy and influential individuals. In Chapter 1, "Imperfect Poet-Critics," I discuss the rise of T. S. Eliot, who quickly came to epitomize the figure of the poet-critic for his contemporaries. Eliot selectively engaged with literary predecessors like Arthur Symons, A. C. Swinburne, and Matthew Arnold in order to craft an argument for poets as the most qualified literary critics, and for criticism as an essential tool of modernism. In a sense, Eliot argued that poets were the aristocrats of criticism, naturally sensitive to superior aesthetic values and uniquely suited to shape literary taste.

But Eliot's aristocracy of sensibility required an aristocracy of wealth to support it: he was still reliant on patrons to fund projects like his little magazine the *Criterion*. Chapter 2, "Picking and Choosing," considers the case of Marianne Moore, who practiced a less confrontational style of criticism than Eliot but more fully embodied the aristocratic poet-critic's ability to intercede between a wealthy patron (in her case Scofield Thayer, the owner and editor of the *Dial*) and the public. Her field of journalistic operations was not the public sphere of critical argument but the editorial, curatorial, and administrative, thus pointing a way forward for ambitious poet-critics in subsequent decades.

Another space in which modernist poet-critics' charisma and credibility were established, aside from the little magazine, was the undergraduate college. Chapter 3, "Student Bodies," begins by assessing Eliot's reputation among elite undergraduates at Oxford and

Cambridge in the 1920s before turning to W. H. Auden, one of Eliot's many student disciples. In his critical essays of the early 1930s and his long poem *The Orators*, Auden began to critique the elite scholastic culture that had produced him and to explore its potential associations with fascism; this was linked to a larger democratic critique of the aristocratic institutional orientation of modernism.

Auden's concern with the connection between aristocratic modernism and authoritarianism was shared by his American contemporary Archibald MacLeish, who is the subject of Chapter 4, "Interrupting the Muse." Although MacLeish began as a mandarin firmly committed to the notion of aesthetic autonomy, he became increasingly political over the course of the 1930s and criticized his fellow modernists for being insufficiently committed to the cause of liberal democracy. MacLeish, more than anyone else, exemplifies the administrative role that the nation-state called on poet-critics to play in the 1930s and 1940s, serving in the Roosevelt administration in key roles, first as librarian of Congress and later as director of the War Department's Office of Facts and Figures.

But government work was not as comfortable a fit for every poet-critic. In the second half of Chapter 4, I turn from MacLeish to Sterling A. Brown in order to demonstrate some of the paradoxes, compromises, and contradictions that poet-critics' service to the nation-state entailed. The case of Brown, who served as editor of Negro affairs for the Federal Writers' Project, demonstrates inherent conflicts in state support for literary production that were intensified by racial tensions and inequalities; the agenda of the New Deal-era welfare state and the agenda of an African American poet-critic like Brown could not easily be brought into alignment.

The book's fifth and final chapter, "The Foundations of Criticism," brings us from the governmental into the philanthropic sector, focusing on an ambitious attempt spearheaded by R. P. Blackmur to secure support for little magazines from the Rockefeller Foundation. Blackmur, as we shall see, was highly skeptical about the adequacy of both the university and the government as institutions of modernism and thus chose to participate in a grand philanthropic experiment. This leads me to consider the role that poet-critics came to play in organized philanthropy and, more broadly, in the "grants economy" and the justification of literature as a social good. Finally, in a brief conclusion titled "With the Program," I analyze two moments in the postwar institutionalization of the poet-critic within the American academy: Auden's Phi Beta Kappa address at Harvard University's 1946 commencement ceremony and the foundation of the Kenyon School of English by John Crowe Ransom in 1948.

Although this book ceases its narrative in the early 1950s, on the eve of various revolutions in poetry (the Beats, the Movement, the New York school) and literary criticism (structuralism, deconstruction, a resurgent Marxism), I hope it will be clear that the landscape designed by and for the modernists is still where contemporary poets, critics, and scholars dwell, even if it is now partially in ruins. The administrative projects undertaken by modernist poet-critics between 1920 and 1950 both underlay the formidable achievements of the Anglo-American literary culture of the subsequent sixty years and produced new problems that we and future generations of poets, critics, and scholars still have to reckon with. If the struggle of the modernists was to make peace with bureaucratic institutions without compromising the purity and quality of their work, the question for those who have come after them has been whether to challenge or sustain that peace. The modernist union of poetry, criticism, and bureaucracy has had many obvious benefits: certainly the levels of comfort, prosperity, and productivity enjoyed by several generations of Anglo-American poets from the postwar era onward as a result of their connection to bureaucratic institutions are nothing to minimize.

But the particular kind of double life that the modernist poet-critics normalized has made it harder to conceive of an autonomous poetic culture that exists apart from the architectonic supports of bureaucratic institutions. In an age of dwindling resources in both the public and private sectors—not to mention rampant populist anti-intellectualism and skepticism even on the part of elites about the value of the humanities—that may be exactly the future that today's poet-critics and scholars most need to imagine, whether they want to or not. It is common enough to complain that American poetry culture, as it exists today, is too exclusive, unequal, or artificial. This is all true, but that culture is also incredibly fragile. Much of what we view as our robust vernacular culture of poetic composition and instruction could easily be decimated with a stroke of an administrator's pen or a change in priorities on the part of a foundation officer. We don't really know what American poetry would look like without the villages, and the village explainers, that have allowed it to thrive. We may yet find out.

1

Imperfect Poet-Critics

IF THERE IS SUCH a thing as a perfect modernist poet-critic, it is probably T. S. Eliot. In his lifetime, certainly, Eliot was regarded as a kind of ideal type. Edmund Wilson's assessment in *Axel's Castle* illustrates the remarkable impression that Eliot's criticism made on his contemporaries. After faulting Ezra Pound for his "scrappy" prose, which is nonetheless "valuable to his generation as polemic, as propaganda and as illuminating casual criticism," Wilson goes on to praise Eliot for "establish[ing] and develop[ing] a distinct reasoned point of view. . . . T. S. Eliot has thought persistently and coherently about the relations between the different phases of human experience, and his passion for proportion and order is reflected in his poems. He is, in his way, a complete man, and . . . it is this intellectual completeness and soundness which has given his rhythm its special prestige."[1]

Wilson's praise of Eliot as a "complete man" is an early example of a topos René Wellek, in his 1970 jeremiad "The Poet as Critic, the Critic as Poet, the Poet-Critic," identifies as intrinsic to the discourse on poet-critics: the "illusion" that "the union of poet and critic . . . restores the original whole man, the *uomo universale* of the Renaissance."[2] A writer like Eliot, who not only wrote criticism as well as poetry but also somehow convinced his readers that the two undertakings were intimately related, was deeply reassuring to skeptics like Wilson who were suspicious of avant-garde experimentation as embodied in controversial figures like Pound and Gertrude

Stein. For Wilson, Eliot's "reasoned" (as opposed to Pound's "casual") criticism provides the security deposit necessary to guarantee his aesthetic of fragmentary obscurity, which might otherwise seem merely perverse. Eliot's "passion for proportion and order," clearly evidenced in his careful critical writing, is somehow "reflected" (though not, of course, directly) in his poems. The overall coherence of Eliot's work is demonstrated not by the poems themselves—which Wilson criticizes as monotonous and morbid—but in the dialectical relation between poetry and criticism, issuing in the satisfyingly "complete" synthesis that is Eliot's persona and career.

From quite early on, then, Eliot's achievement was seen as twofold: he justified the practice of poetry, and the perspective of the practicing poet, to critics (both journalistic and academic); and he justified the practice of criticism to poets, in part by demonstrating the professional power and autonomy that mastery of critical writing could win them. From the early 1920s onward, even those poet-critics who directly opposed or disagreed with Eliot's views were performing a social role he exemplified and helped codify for the culture at large.

❧❧❧

The journalistic context of Eliot's early essays is easily forgotten now that texts like "Hamlet and His Problems" and "Tradition and the Individual Talent" have found their way into millions of syllabi. But this context is crucial to any understanding of Eliot's critical project in the late 1910s and early 1920s. The field of English criticism, at the time Eliot entered it in the mid-1910s, was still dominated, as it had been for decades, by competition among professional journalists, moonlighting academic scholars of literature, and members of the political intelligentsia.[3] Eliot, following his mentor, Pound, launches his initial attack on this culture from an aestheticist position: he declares, in no uncertain terms, that all these parties (journalists, academics, and pundits) are incompetent to judge literary value, and that what they are producing is not really criticism. The superiority of the practitioner-critic had long been a standard theme of Pound's, but for the early Eliot it is practically an obsession. In an unsigned piece for the *Egoist* in April 1918, he defends literary professionalism against journalistic dilettantism: "The opposite of the professional is not the dilettante, the elegant amateur, the dabbler who in fact only attests the existence of the specialist. The opposite of the professional, the enemy, is the man of mixed motives."[4]

Who were the real professionals when it came to poetry, then? Poets. The claim of Eliot's earliest criticism is that none of the extant professional critics are able to actually read poetry; only poets can do it properly, without the "mixed motives" he had earlier ascribed to journalists. In 1920 he concluded his essay "Imperfect Critics" with the claim that "the creative artist in England finds himself compelled, or at least tempted, to spend much of his time and energy in criticism that he might reserve for the perfecting of his proper work: simply because there is no one else to do it."[5] In fact, there were plenty of people to do it, and plenty who were doing it. But Eliot's claim was that what they called "criticism" was, in reality, nothing of the sort.

Rather than simply enter into competition, then, Eliot wanted to change the rules of the game that was being played, tilting the table to his own advantage. Instead of a few poets having to prove themselves intelligent enough to moonlight as literary critics, the assumption would henceforth be that virtually any poet who deserves the name has truer aesthetic instincts about literature and literary value than virtually any critic. Rather than struggling to legitimate his own talents and cultural capital, Eliot put his rivals on the defensive, demanding that they prove themselves worthy of the right to enter into discussion with him.[6]

It is with this agenda in mind that Eliot, in the series of essays that began his 1920 collection *The Sacred Wood*, self-consciously assumes the mantle of both poet-critic and (to adapt his description of Matthew Arnold) "propagandist for poet-criticism." Beginning with his piece on "Swinburne and the Elizabethans" in the *Athenaeum* of September 19, 1919, Eliot writes almost exclusively about poets who had also produced a substantial body of critical writing, including Ben Jonson, William Blake, John Dryden, and Arthur Symons. At the same time, he insists repeatedly on the superiority of criticism written by poets to that of nonpractitioners (having already spoken, as early as 1916, of "those flashes of insight which arise in the comments of one creative artist upon another").[7] These concerns culminate in the essays that became the first two items in *The Sacred Wood* (barring a short preface, to which I will return later): "The Perfect Critic" and "Imperfect Critics." As their titles suggest, these pieces provide a kind of rapid survey of literary criticism up to Eliot's time, with the goal of orienting the future practice of Eliot and others. The words "perfect" and "imperfect" already announce this teleological aim, distinguishing Eliot's essays from a mere chronicle along the lines of Saintsbury's *History of Literary Criticism*. He is proceeding by process of elimination.

In "The Perfect Critic" Eliot considers a number of candidates for the titular honor, inspecting Coleridge, Arnold, Horace, Dryden, Thomas Campion, Rémy de Gourmont, and François de La Rochefoucauld in turn before finally settling on good old Aristotle, whom he praises as the most "scientific" and "intelligent" of literary critics.[8] Although Aristotle provides the safe classical point of origin toward which the retrospective investigation of "The Perfect Critic" is ultimately directed, Eliot is not really recommending a more Aristotelian criticism. His interest is not in Aristotle's method—since, as he memorably put it, "the only method is to be very intelligent"—but in the quality of his mind. Eliot's rather rote celebration of Aristotle, besides being an early example of his lifelong fetishization of "classicism" and "the classic," introduces a psychological approach to criticism that runs throughout *The Sacred Wood*: he is interested, above all, not in critical texts or even critical theories but critical minds.

Among the poet-critics who fail to measure up to Aristotle in "The Perfect Critic" is Arthur Symons, one of the leading lights of the fading Symbolist movement, whose *Studies in Elizabethan Drama* was the occasion for the essay, and whose *The Symbolist Movement in Literature*, published in 1899, had been a crucial text for Eliot's early poetic development. Describing his initial encounter with the latter text, Eliot (using the royal "we," as was his wont) writes that "we remember that book as an introduction to wholly new feelings, as a revelation. After we have read Verlaine and Laforgue and Rimbaud and return to Mr. Symons' book, we may find that our own impressions dissent from his. The book has not, perhaps, a permanent value for the one reader, but it has led to results of permanent importance for him."[9] Given the faintness of the praise Eliot accords Symons here (his book is not valuable, but "it has led to results" of value), it can be easy to miss the significance of the terms of praise. Eliot's portrait of Symons conforms to the general pattern of his treatment of other predecessor poet-critics, whose ideas are typically dismissed or disparaged even as their style and sensibility are complimented. Their minds, he suggests over and over, were exceptional, but the works those minds produced were sadly not; with a bit more effort and strength of character and philosophical rigor, they really could have done much better.

It is this rhetorical move that explains Eliot's continual recourse, in an essay that generally recommends "scientific" criticism, to one science in particular: psychology. He treats poor Symons less like a respected elder than like an experimental research subject: "He, if anyone, would be said to expose a sensitive and cultivated mind . . . before an 'object'; and his criticism, if anyone's, would be said to exhibit to us, like the plate, the faithful record of the impressions, more numerous and more refined than our own, upon a mind more sensitive than our own."[10] This is essentially a scientistic restatement of the basic assumptions of Paterian aestheticism: here, the "sensitive and cultivated mind" of the poet-critic is valuable first and foremost as a record of sense-data, even if the possessor of that instrument is incapable of interpreting that data interestingly.

The disparagement of Symons is cruel enough that one can get distracted from the implicit, and important, claim that Eliot is making for poet-critics as aesthetic receptors. The first advantage the poet-critic has over all other commentators is a psychological, as opposed to a cognitive, one: whether or not the ideas or beliefs that poets consciously hold about literature happen to be coherent or true, Eliot suggests, they are still constitutionally capable of experiencing the effects of poetry at a level of sophistication unavailable to the general reader.

This psychological theory of the poet as a "perfect" or "natural" critic is extended to another problematic aestheticist predecessor when Eliot makes the rather bizarre comment, later in the same essay, that "Swinburne found an adequate outlet for the creative impulse in his poetry; and none of it was forced back and out through his critical prose." This surprising recourse to something like a Freudian theory of repression—in which a psychic "impulse," for lack of an "adequate outlet," gets sublimated and expressed in compensatory form—serves to shore up a sense of the poet-critic as inherently superior to, even healthier than, the nonpoet: "This gives us an intimation why the artist is—each within his own limitations— oftenest to be depended upon as a critic; his criticism will be criticism, and not the satisfaction of a suppressed creative wish—which, in most other persons, is apt to interfere fatally."[11] This, in Dr. Eliot's expert diagnosis, is what has happened to Arthur Symons: "I imagine . . . that Mr. Symons is far more disturbed, far more profoundly affected, by his reading than was Swinburne, who responded rather by a violent and immediate and comprehensive burst of admiration which may have left him internally unchanged. The disturbance in Mr. Symons is almost, but not quite, to the point of creating; the reading sometimes fecundates his emotions to produce something new which is not criticism, but is not the expulsion, the ejection, the birth of creativeness."[12] The rhetoric of "disturbance" again suggests a psychoanalytic, or at least therapeutic, discourse. The "perfect" poet-critic is the one who can create and criticize equally well, but who never gets the two procedures confused.

In essence, this whole rococo line of thought is just a reformulation of the cliché that all critics secretly want to be practitioners, and that their frustration and envy of the failed creative artist inevitably interferes with their objective judgment. This was already an *idée reçue* by the end of the eighteenth century, and the dubious "psychological" foundation Eliot gives it here can't completely disguise its banality. Tactically, though, the theory developed in "The Perfect Critic" is brilliant. Eliot's assumption that there are basic differences in the types of minds that experience poetry allows him to argue something paradoxical: that an accomplished and successful poet is more capable of being objective, of being a pure critic, than most other persons. Thus he ingeniously turned what might have been a disadvantage for the poet-critic (deep personal investment in the literary field, which one might reason-ably see as a barrier to objectivity) into an advantage. In a strategic reversal, the poet-critics who might have been open to accusations of being "[men] of mixed motives"—promoting their own and their friends' work, for instance, as Pound was frequently charged with doing—are presented as the only true professionals, disinterested because they have already discharged their creative energy elsewhere.

∽◌∾ ∽◌∾ ∽◌∾

In *The Sacred Wood*, "The Perfect Critic" is immediately followed by a companion piece titled "Imperfect Critics." Here Swinburne appears again, this time as the patient etherized on the table. Eliot takes the great Pre-Raphaelite to task for his self-indulgent prose style but notes that his "style has one positive merit: it allows us to know that Swinburne was writing not to establish a critical reputa-tion, not to instruct a docile public, but as a poet his notes upon poets whom he admired. And whatever our opinion of Swinburne's verse, the notes upon poets by a poet of Swinburne's dimensions must be read with attention and respect."[13] Once again the prac-ticing poet is presented as though he were a natural critic, one who possesses an innate advantage over the competition simply by virtue of being able to read and experience poetry at a higher level. And, again, Eliot suggests that the critic's status as practicing poet, far from presenting a danger of bias or partiality (a craven concern for "reputation," whether critical or poetic), is actually the ultimate proof of his disinterestedness.

In "Imperfect Critics," however, the terms of approbation are less scientific than they are ethical. The work of criticism is taken to be an act of generosity, founded on a kind of professional or vocational solidarity, "notes upon poets whom he [as a poet] admired." It would seem that the sensitive poet-critic is disinclined to serve a peda-gogical function; he is writing "not to instruct a docile public" but only for himself and his friends alone. (He is not a village explainer in Stein's sense.) Eliot approves of this to an extent, insofar as the private ethic of pleasure and generosity forecloses the possibility of using criticism for propagandistic or self-promotional purposes. But a purely personal economy of mutual gift giving, whatever its value in safeguarding against impure forms of interest, runs the risk of making criticism into nothing more than shop talk among poets. Poet-critics like Swinburne, brilliant as they are, show no interest in deriving theories and principles from their observations that can be used to guide the critical inquiries of others or learned by the layman in order to establish a foundation for literary taste. This fault is enough to disqualify Swinburne from the inner circle of critical perfection: "With all the justness of his judgment . . . Swinburne is an appreciator and not a critic. . . . [W]e cannot say that his thinking is faulty or perverse—up to the point at which it is thinking. But Swinburne stops thinking just at the moment when we are most zealous to go on. And this arrest, while it does not vitiate his work, makes it an introduction rather than a statement."[14] Like Symons, Swinburne is praised for his "sensibility" but faulted for his "thinking" ("up to the point at which it is thinking": ouch). But again, by pointing to what past poet-critics haven't done, Eliot indicates by implication what they *could* do. By regretting Swinburne's preference for appreciating poetry rather than analyzing it, he executes a subtle but very significant shift. He goes from recommending poets for tasks currently performed by journalists and book reviewers (evaluation and publicity) to suggesting that they might be capable of one historically performed by scholars and even philosophers (theoretical justification and the formulation of rational principles). It is the language of formal logic, not aesthetics or even ethics, that Eliot uses to claim that, whether or not it yielded practical results, such criticism would at least demonstrate "the movements of an important mind groping toward important conclusions": "As it is, there are to be no conclusions, except that Elizabethan literature is very great, and that you can have pleasure and even ecstasy from it, because a sensitive poetic talent has had the experience. One is in risk of becoming fatigued by a hubbub that does not march; the drum is beaten, but the procession does not advance."[15] As with Symons, Eliot praises Swinburne's perceptiveness and disinterestedness while regretting his "sensitive" self-absorption and his lack of ultimate purpose.

Eliot's rhetoric of "advancement" here recalls the military parlance of the avant-garde so prevalent on the Continental literary scene by 1920 (and beloved by, among others, Pound), and of which he was otherwise skeptical. But whatever his conception of modernism as a quasi-political project, Eliot's point here is clear. He is regretting past poet-critics' intellectual deficits, their lack of social efficacy, and their inability to establish any permanent movement or tradition. The exquisite, temporary aestheticism of poet-critics like Swinburne and Symons, however fine, cannot be the basis for a more permanent, rational justification of the practice of poetry, a justification that would establish poetry as a common good for people less sensitive than themselves. "As it is, there are to be no conclusions" is an assessment that links Eliot's disapproval of the poet-critics' style of argument (no logical conclusions are reached) to their sterility as aesthetic examples and the social temporariness of their literary positions (it is not possible to conclude, or even to continue, what they started). The history of poet-critics looks, to the young Eliot at the dawn of the 1920s, like a history of beautiful dead ends.

❧ ❧ ❧

Eliot was not the first poet-critic to talk like this, of course. In the 1860s, Matthew Arnold formulated a broadly similar argument, focused not on poet-critics in particular but on English literary and intellectual culture generally. Eliot was aware that he was retracing Arnold's steps—this is why he included "The Second-Order Mind," first published in the *Dial* in 1920, as an untitled preface to *The Sacred Wood*—but he insists that this time, it will be different. In a remarkable feat of recontextualization, Eliot makes Arnold not a role model but a cautionary tale, an example of a well-meaning poet-critic who allowed his critical intelligence to overwhelm his poetic talent.

Just as "The Perfect Critic" and "Imperfect Critics" were, in part, reckonings with the legacies of Symons and Swinburne, "The Second-Order Mind" explicitly declares itself an attempt to come to terms with Arnold. From the essay's first sentence, Eliot frames his remarks as a long-awaited rapprochement with an old nemesis: "To anyone who is at all capable of experiencing the pleasures of justice, it is gratifying to be able to make amends to a writer whom one has vaguely depreciated for years. . . . I hope that now, on rereading some of his prose with more care, I can better appreciate his position. And what makes Arnold seem all the more remarkable is, that if he were our exact contemporary, he would find all his labour to perform again."[16] These belated "amends" (borrowing the topos of reconciliation with a problematic literary predecessor from Pound's apostrophe to Walt Whitman in his poem "A Pact") engages with Arnold by historicizing him, dealing not just with his work but, quite literally, with his "position," which in context implies a historical situation as well as a set of philosophical beliefs. This new, more just way of appreciating Arnold's legacy, focusing on the entirety of his "labour" rather than the literal content of his critical writings, proceeds by sympathetic projection, drawing an implicit analogy between Arnold's late Victorian heyday and Eliot's Georgian moment. (Note that Eliot instructs his reader to imagine Arnold as "our exact contemporary.") It put Arnold, in fact, more or less in the position of Eliot circa 1920: an ambitious young poet-critic making a survey of the present and the past and emerging deeply disappointed. To grasp the relationship between the two poet-critics in their respective historical situations, we can look at a passage that Eliot quotes a little later in this essay from Arnold's "The Function of Criticism at the Present Time":

> It has long seemed to me that the burst of creative activity in our literature, through the first quarter of the century, had about it in fact something premature; and that from this cause its productions are doomed, most of them, in spite of the sanguine hopes which accompanied and do still accompany them, to prove hardly more lasting than the productions of far less splendid epochs. And this prematureness comes from having proceeded without having its proper data, without sufficient material to work with. In other words, the English poetry of the first quarter of this century, with plenty of energy, plenty of creative force, did not know enough.[17]

This is less a formal or ideological critique than a practical one, expressed in the language of science or even administration: Arnold reprimands the Romantics for "proceed[ing] without . . . proper data." In quoting this passage when and where he does, Eliot is implicitly comparing Arnold's account of the English Romantics and the emerging popular consensus on Anglo-American modernism. Each movement had the "energy" but not the "material," the force but not the culture, and because of this, their "productions are doomed" not to be "lasting."

But rather than merely repeating Arnold's claim for the scholastic imposition of Hellenistic culture as a correcting force for impetuous literary genius, Eliot turns the quotation back on its author, reflecting on Arnold's ultimate failure to make his critical productions last: "[Arnold's] judgment of the Romantic Generation has not, so far as I know, ever been successfully controverted; and it has not, so far as I know, ever made very much impression on popular opinion. Once a poet is accepted, his reputation is seldom disturbed, for better or worse. So little impression has Arnold's opinion made, that his statement will probably be as true of the first quarter of the twentieth century as it was of the nineteenth."[18]

This is a critique of Arnold very much in the spirit of Arnold himself. One popular post-Victorian conception of Arnold was that he sacrificed his poetic gift in order to devote himself to social criticism and the cause of "culture." He thus stands (and not only for Eliot) as the epitome of the poet-critic's potential martyrdom to the "journeyman-work of literature" (to borrow a phrase from Arnold's "The Literary Influence of Academies"). Eliot, attracted as he was to the notion of self-sacrifice, is prepared to respect Arnold's grand renunciation, but he still persists in pointing out that the critical and cultural project for which he sacrificed his poetry failed. "Culture," in Arnold's exalted sense, is no more secure in the England of the 1920s than it had been in the 1860s, when Arnold published *Essays in Criticism*. "A moderate number of people have engaged in what is called 'critical' writing," Eliot notes, "but no conclusion is any more solidly established than it was in 1865."[19] This is why Arnold, were he magically resurrected in 1920, "would find all his labour to perform again." What Eliot points to here is not the quality of the labor, or even the success or failure of the effort in its time, but the fact that it has not been permanently effective. The regret is double: that the truly energetic poetic movements (like the Romantics and the "men of 1914") lacked the necessary critical culture to focus their creative potential, and that when that focusing culture does arrive—always after the fact—it is largely wasted because it lacks the institutional means to ensure the permanent maintenance of its achievements. As it is, there are to be no conclusions; the drum is beaten, but the procession does not advance.

In such a situation, it is necessary for the responsible poet to become not just a critic but a "propagandist for criticism": to justify the need for criticism, and for people of aesthetic sensitivity (i.e., poets) to practice it. In Eliot's view, Arnold fulfilled this melancholy obligation, but the task of being a propagandist kept him from the actual, constructive practice of criticism (which, in turn, kept him from his poetry): "In a society in which the arts were seriously studied, in which the art of writing was respected, Arnold might have become a critic. . . . In *Culture and Anarchy*, in *Literature and Dogma*, Arnold was not occupied so much in establishing a criticism as in attacking the uncritical. The difference is that while in constructive work something can be done, destructive work must incessantly be repeated."[20]

In Eliot's view, Arnold's propaganda for criticism, however noble and necessary, was a waste of his talents, not just because it kept him from poetry or led him to enter into matters he was not qualified to address, but because it was only temporarily useful. As a program of action, it entailed primarily "destructive work"—the destruction of utilitarian misconceptions that literature should serve clearly defined rational and social ends—and this work, even when effective, does not last but "must incessantly be repeated." Thus, criticism becomes a kind of Sisyphean labor, a continual and futile "correcting of taste," rather than an acculturating force directed toward the development of a lasting tradition. And "culture," as both Arnold and Eliot see it, entails more than correction.

⚜ ⚜ ⚜

So far, Eliot's engagement with Arnold resembles his engagements with Symons and Swinburne: deference and respect giving way to disappointment. But it differs from them in that it faults Arnold not for his failure as a critic but for his success. It is as if the example of Arnold had presented Eliot with a new kind of sociological concern, one not about the exclusion of poets from the sphere of criticism but about their exploitation and exhaustion within it. Having established that poets are better suited to supply literary criticism than the philosophers, academics, and professional journalists who had been supplying it, Eliot realizes that he has transferred a tremendous amount of labor to the poet. If "the creative artist . . . finds himself compelled . . . to spend much of his time and energy in criticism . . . simply because there is no one else to do it," as Eliot suggests at the end of "Imperfect Critics," then we have arrived at a whole new definition of "the creative artist" or, at least, a new job description, one that involves "compulsion" and, thus, unfreedom. Such an arrangement might be good for the art of poetry as a whole, in that it raises critical standards, and for the art of criticism, in that it brings it much closer to grasping the autonomous logic of genuine art. But it is at best a mixed blessing for actual poet-critics, who are now burdened with a whole new set of tasks and responsibilities and a whole new literary mode to master.

Eliot gives the pithiest expression of this dilemma in an uncollected essay of 1920, "A Brief Treatise on the Criticism of Poetry," wherein he laments that "either a reviewer is a bad writer and bad critic, and he ought not to be allowed to intervene between books and the public; or he is a good writer and good critic, and therefore ought not to be occupied in writing about inferior books."[21] Poets make perfect critics, in part because (since their passions are expended in creation, not in criticism) they are disinterested; but, by the same logic, they ought to have no real interest in pursuing criticism in the first place, but should prefer to focus their energies solely on creation. Too much diversion of that passionate energy, as in the case of Arnold, would inevitably make them into very imperfect poets.

On the one hand, Eliot wants to reserve a privileged place in the English critical sphere for poet-critics; on the other, he wants to protect them from shouldering too much of the burden of critical labor. (A village explainer may be excellent if you're a village, but not if you're an explainer.) Having established the difference between poets and other kinds of critics, then, he needs to make a further distinction, within the fraction of poets who operate as poet-critics, to keep the truly individual talents from being crushed by an excess of critical labor. This produces a new set of categories for Eliot to manipulate in addition to "poet" and "critic":

> Not only is the critic tempted outside of criticism. The criticism proper betrays such poverty of ideas and such atrophy of sensibility that men who ought to preserve their critical ability for the improvement of their own creative work are tempted into criticism. I do not intend from this the usually silly inference that the "creative" gift is "higher" than the critical. When one creative mind is better than another, the reason often is that the better is the more critical. But the great bulk of the work of criticism could be done by minds of the second order, and it is just these minds of the second order that are difficult to find.[22]

Fittingly for a man who would soon declare himself "a Royalist in politics," Eliot's vision is hierarchical: there are minds of the first order, minds of the second order, and presumably many lower orders beneath that. But he was also a modernist and a man of his time, and as he contemplated some kind of reform of literary culture, he saw only one medium as appropriate for the efficient organization of second-order minds: the little magazine.

⁓⁓ ⁓⁓ ⁓⁓

Although his work gave many others inspiration and hope, it should be acknowledged that Eliot's view of the poet-critic's role within literary culture was largely pessimistic. Pound, an optimist of sorts, imagined a heroic intellectual elite with boundless energy that would both produce and interpret culture. Eliot foresaw, instead, the resentment and ennui of a class of writers who were attempting to carry simultaneously the banners of two traditions—the critical and the poetic—that would, in a more rational society, have been kept distinct. The second-order minds should be writing the criticism, he thought, while the first-order minds handled the poetry. No Matthew Arnold should need to waste his powers on admonitory essays or, even worse, on administrative work.

As so often with Eliot, this apparently abstract idea has personal roots. In the late 1910s and early 1920s Eliot was deriving the bulk of his income from freelance book reviewing; his correspondence of the period contains endless complaints about the sapping of his energies and the pettiness of his daily responsibilities. In 1922 these themes of fatigue and decline would be blown up to mythological scale in *The Waste Land*. But I will conclude by looking at an earlier poem, one published in the same year as *The Sacred Wood*. Let's stay with 1919–1920, the years of Eliot's most significant and feverish critical output, and a poem that reflects many of these anxieties about labor, exhaustion, and oversensitivity as if through a glass darkly: "Gerontion."[23]

"Gerontion" is a "critical" poem in a formal sense. Composed near the peak of Eliot's productivity as a freelance critic, it incorporates a number of allusions to books he had recently reviewed, including A. C. Benson's *Edward Fitzgerald*, the sermons of Lancelot Andrewes, and *The Education of Henry Adams*, as well as various Jacobean and Elizabethan plays that would feed into his magisterial 1919 essay "'Rhetoric' and Poetic Drama." In addition to these references, however, there is a deeper sense in which "Gerontion" is about criticism and the dangers it poses to poetry. It can be read not as a metaphysical reflection on the nightmare of history but as the coded recounting of a specific historical nightmare from which Eliot was trying to awake.

Here, as elsewhere, the oft-remarked difference in tone between Eliot's fragmented, tortured verse and confident critical prose should not lead us to posit an antinomy between them. What Eliot was worrying about in his criticism and what he was worrying about in his poetry were in fact, and as usual, the same thing: the relations between successive literary generations, the weaknesses and strengths of his own position in the literary field, and the besetting difficulties of cultural transmission and preservation that he had recently placed under the heading "tradition." The difference is that what Eliot was certain about, or endeavored to appear certain about, in his criticism remained a question for him in his poetry. We might say that in Eliot's criticism he contrived to find plausible solutions, whereas in the poetry he was more interested in dramatizing the questions.

"Gerontion," like "The Love Song of J. Alfred Prufrock" and many of Eliot's other early poems, is a kind of dramatic monologue; the title is almost always taken by commentators to be the speaker's name, although this fact does not seem evident from the text. Instead, the title floats above the poem, naming not so much the speaker as the whole social climate he inhabits. (In addition to its primary meaning of "old man," "Gerontion" is also a near homonym for "generation," a then-novel sociological term that crops up often in Eliot's critical writing of this period.) It is customary to remark that the voice that speaks "Gerontion" is left indistinct in its particulars: about the only thing we know about him is that he is old, or at least perceives himself as such. But this sense of age takes its meaning only from an implied comparison to others who are younger, just as Eliot can describe himself as "the ageing" only in relation to a new generation of literary recruits. The poem's first words, "Here I am, an old man," introduce this ambiguity immediately: is "Gerontion" the "I" or the "here"? Is "an old man" who he is, or is it where he is? (This is not as unidiomatic as it sounds: we do speak of "getting to a certain age.") To put it another way, if all we know about the speaker is that he is old, is that a property of his being, or is it a function of his contingent position in time and space?

We can tell, too, that the speaker of "Gerontion" is in a position of extreme dependence on others. The poem's opening lines describe him as "an old man, read to by a boy"; later, we are told of a "woman [who] keeps the kitchen." Age, as often in Eliot, is associated here with helplessness, inactivity, and passive contemplation, and the speaker's weakness is further signaled by his evocation of a recently completed battle, in which he did not take part: "I was neither at the hot gates/Nor fought in the warm rain/Nor knee deep in the salt marsh, heaving a cutlass,/Bitten by flies, fought." "Old man" and "boy" are alike excluded from this field of masculine action (too old and too young to fight, respectively). The important distinction is thus not so much between youth and age as between those who participate in epochal battles and those who are (or feel) excluded from them. Thus the epigraph, from Shakespeare's *Measure for Measure*: "Thou hast nor youth nor age/But as it were an after dinner sleep/Dreaming of both." The speaker of "Gerontion" is a noncombatant, a dreamer as opposed to a doer: a sensitive soul and little more.

It is in the third stanza that "Gerontion" begins to coalesce, in emotional and rhetorical power if not in scenario. Although he is excluded from the struggles that make history, the speaker realizes that he may have the power to shape the narrative of those struggles: "Think now/History has many cunning passages, contrived corridors/And issues." His power, in other words, may not be creative but critical: a power not to make things happen but to explain what has happened and what may come next. The literary pun on "passages" is reinforced by the ambiguity of the word "issues," which suggests numbers of periodicals as well as social and political problems. The speaker of "Gerontion" realizes that, in trying to clarify issues, he is capable of engendering "supple confusions" that distract from what was originally desired or intended; in this way, "the giving famishes the craving," and he leaves his hearers, or readers, unsatisfied. He worries, too, that he hasn't arrived on the scene of criticism in a timely fashion, that he's either "too soon" or "too late" to intervene effectively. He is anxious about what can and can't be transmitted to the coming generation, and troubled by an understanding that whatever is passed along may not be what the speaker intended to transmit: "Unnatural vices/Are fathered by our heroism. Virtues/Are forced upon us by our impudent crimes."

"Gerontion" thus expresses Eliot's fear of ending up like Arnold, with his creative energies dissipated and "all his labour to perform again":

> Think at last
> We have not reached conclusion, when I
> Stiffen in a rented house. Think at last
> I have not made this show purposelessly

An overwhelming desire to "reach conclusion," to "think at last," suffuses all of Eliot's early writing on poet-critics, as does his immense frustration with the generations of brilliant minds before him who have "made [their] show purposelessly." Eliot the rationalist, the conservative, the university-trained philosopher, is haunted by

the desire to "think at last," to transcend the fleeting moment of
aesthetic sensibility, to produce that which can be effectively reproduced: a lasting, definitive, transmissible tradition.

That such a "show" might be "purposeless" is a tragic thought,
but an even greater tragedy looms in "Gerontion." This is the prospect of losing one's feeling for poetry—here personified as a beloved
"you"—by giving oneself over too completely to the "terror" of
critical inquiry:

> I that was near your heart was removed therefrom
> To lose beauty in terror, terror in inquisition.
> I have lost my passion: why should I need to keep it
> Since what is kept must be adulterated?
> I have lost my sight, smell, hearing, taste and touch:
> How should I use them for your closer contact?

This is the most straightforwardly lyrical passage in the poem, and
it voices the most purely poetic part of Eliot's character, the part that
fears that criticism will dull his aesthetic sensitivity precisely by
trying to prolong it, since "what is kept must be adulterated." When
the speaker laments that he has lost his "sight, smell, hearing, taste
and touch," the fourth term is the one we should emphasize most:
taste, at once the poet-critic's ace in the hole and Achilles's heel.
Taste is what distinguishes the poet-critic—what else should we call
Symons and Swinburne's exquisite sensibilities?—and it is what he
has to bring to market, a commodity carried within the self ("near
your heart"). But it is an asset that is exploited at the possible risk of
estranging oneself from "closer contact" with poetry itself. The last
stanza of "Gerontion" imagines exactly this risk:

> These with a thousand small deliberations
> Protract the profit of their chilled delirium,
> Excite the membrane, when the sense has cooled,
> With pungent sauces, multiply variety
> In a wilderness of mirrors.

It is precisely the job of the professional literary critic to make
"a thousand small deliberations" that "protract the profit" of the

"chilled delirium" of individual aesthetic response, trying to keep the experience of poetry alive past its natural time in order to analyze and draw conclusions from it. Again, as in "The Perfect Critic," aesthetic sensibility belongs to the moment, the past, while abstract thought and argument, like "protract[ed] profit," belongs to the future. It is the unique role of criticism to bridge the two, but it comes at a price: the act of intellectualizing what has temporarily "excite[d] the membrane" may "cool" the critic's senses. The poet-critic erects a bridge to the future at the cost of consigning authentic aesthetic experience to the past.

The immense weariness of Eliot's poetic voice is intimately bound up with this sacrifice. It is the voice of a writer who feels called on to do too much, to do things that are against his true nature, and whose lyrical achievements have come about only through hard labor and stolen time. His poetry is designed to sound as if it were the product of an intense internal struggle, as though it were an attempt to wring feeling out of an exhausted shell. It is this affect, more than any particular principle or methodology, that Eliot bequeathed to the poet-critics of his generation and the next: the glamour of overwork, of near exhaustion, and of sacrifice; a portrait of the artist as an old man.

2

Picking and Choosing

IN JANUARY 1919, Marianne Moore wrote a letter—the first of many—to her fellow poet-critic Ezra Pound.[1] Pound had initiated the correspondence after encountering some work Moore had submitted for publication in the *Little Review*, seeing in her work some similarities to his own. After politely deflating most of his conjectures ("The resemblance of my progress to your beginnings is but an accident so far as I can see"), she makes so bold as to advance an unsolicited opinion of Pound himself: "I have taken great pleasure in both your prose and your verse, but it is what my mother terms the saucy parts, which have most fixed my attention. In 1911, my mother and I were some months in England and happening into Elkin Matthews's shop, were shown photographs of you which we were much pleased to see. I like a fight but I admit that I have at times objected to your promptness with the cudgels. I say this merely to be honest."[2]

The whole passage has a typically Moorish ambiguity of tone—the attention she pays to Pound and his work is decorous, flirtatious, and disapproving in equal measure—but the phrase that jumps out is the penultimate one, which characterizes not Pound but Moore herself: "I like a fight but I admit that I have at times objected to your promptness with the cudgels." This qualified, partially self-negating criticism encapsulates a characteristic mode of Moore's writing, what I will call her "antagonism toward agonism." This is not the same as a simple abhorrence of confrontation or violence; after all, Moore admits that she does "like a fight" and is, not

incidentally, picking one here—and with a formidable opponent—
by objecting to Pound's aggressive behavior. But the fact that Moore,
at this relatively early stage of the development of modernism and
of her career, felt the need to register an objection, not to any particular attack of Pound's but to his tendency to attack in general, is
significant.

Moore's early tête-à-tête with Pound provides a rather neat and
surprisingly early indication of the tenor of their subsequent
relationship—they would not meet in person until 1939—and of
her relationship to her majority-male modernist cohort as a whole.
As with Pound, so it was with poet-critics like William Carlos
Williams, Richard Aldington, and Eliot, all writers whose vitality
and engagement Moore admired but whose tendency toward aggression she could not. Moore had much invested in being regarded as a
peer by these writers (as, for the most part, she was), and she recognized that these men showed their mutual regard in large part by arguing passionately with one another. But she never fit easily into their
quarrelsome company. Her criticism, unlike that of her contemporaries, seems allergic to argument, reluctant to take up or defend abstract positions, and fearful of negative evaluations and judgments.

But although she was obviously a modernist despite her reluc-
tance to disparage or abandon the literary modes of the nineteenth
century, Moore was just as obviously a full-fledged poet-critic. Her
collected critical prose fills many more pages than either Williams's
or Wallace Stevens's, for instance, and, as many have noted, seems
more of a piece with her poetry than that of most modernists. A
random sentence of Moore's—"The acknowledgment of our debt to
the imagination, constitutes perhaps, its positive value," for instance, or "Ecstasy affords the occasion and expediency determines
the form"—could just as easily be drawn from her criticism as her
poetry; the two corpora mirror, complement, and inform each other
almost perfectly.[3]

Indeed, early assessments of Moore's poetry often refers to its
"critical" qualities. Mark Van Doren, for instance, reviewing Moore
alongside Edna St. Vincent Millay and Anna Wickham in the *Nation*
under the heading "Women of Wit," writes: "For better or worse,
these women have contracted marriages with wit, have committed

themselves to careers of brains. . . . [Their poetry] is independent, *critical*, and keen, a product oftener of the faculties than of the nerves and heart; it is feminine; it is fearless; it is fresh."[4] Similarly, Louis Untermeyer, in a 1923 piece titled "Poetry or Wit?," speaks of Moore's "highly intellectualized dissertations in the form of poetry" and states that "all of her work displays a surface of flickering irony, a nimble sophistication beneath which glitter the depths of a cool and continually *critical* mind."[5]

As these excerpts suggest, an implied contrast between "critical" and "lyrical" poetry—already shadowed by an equivalent contrast between "masculine" and "feminine" temperaments—was crucial to Moore's early reception.[6] Some commentators even go so far as to suggest that Moore is claiming the wrong genre for her work. Untermeyer, for example, finds that "practically all the contents of *Poems* are essays in the disguise of verse, arguments or statements which seem continually to be seeking their prose origins. . . . [T]he critical faculty predominates. . . . [O]ne finds it difficult to understand why this analyst writes so little in what seems to be her native medium."[7] Untermeyer's dismissive assessment of Moore as being out of her "native medium" betrays some of the familiar modernist suspicion about feminine writing, but with the terms oddly reversed: although modernist-era critics rejected much writing by women as being insufficiently tough or intellectual, Moore's work was taken to task as too clinical, too analytical, too oriented toward "arguments" and "statements" as opposed to the cognitively vague lyric utterances expected of a turn-of-the-century poetess.[8]

While Moore's poetry was frequently faulted (and also, on occasion, admired) for its cold, critical, even unlyrical objectivity, her critical writing was often accused of the opposite crime: of being too sensitive, or impressionistic, or "poetic" in a stigmatized, feminized sense. Even otherwise admiring readers frequently advances this charge against Moore. Donald Hall, for example, describes her critical pieces as "impressionistic and unaimed," and Bernard Engle damns them with faint praise by calling them "graceful presentations of observations and impressions, the kind of statement one might expect from a good reader rather than from a professional critic."[9] While her poetry was often criticized as too intellectual and argumentative, Moore's criticism tended to be seen as just the opposite: "graceful" and sensitive but lacking in intellectual rigor, innocuous and a little old-fashioned, and fatally reluctant to advance clear positions or offer confident negative judgments.

Perhaps the harshest assessment of Moore's criticism along these masculinist lines is also one of the earliest, published by Gorham B. Munson in his 1928 book *Destinations* while Moore was still serving as editor of the *Dial*:

> The critic must be ambitious and Miss Moore is not. She attempts to make no more than a sensitive impressionistic sketch of her reading, a sketch that is always liberally studded with quotations from the author under review, and carries a valuable sentence or two of acute technical understanding for good measure. The quotations are ably selected for the object she has in mind, which is to give the "flavor" of the author. But, after all, the "flavor" is *in* the book and each reader of it may garner his own impressions. The critic must do more than that. At any rate, he should not be backward about handling ideas.[10]

In contrast to an ideal "ambitious" critic (conspicuously gendered male, as are the "poet" and the "editor" elsewhere in Munson's essay), Moore is "no more" than "sensitive" and "impressionistic" and is by implication "backward" when it comes to the supra-aesthetic business of "handling ideas." The physical and the metaphysical come together here: ideas are a kind of cargo that only men are strong enough to handle, whereas direct quotation—Moore's critical technique of choice—amounts to little more than a feminine rearrangement of furniture.

It is important to see that these symmetrical tendencies in Moore's reception—the tendency to view her poetry as unusually (or fatally) critical and the tendency to view her criticism as unusually (or fatally) poetic"—are more than misunderstandings; in fact, they point to something that later and otherwise more sympathetic and sophisticated readings of Moore's poetry and criticism have neglected.

This picture of Moore as at once too critical to be a poet and too poetic to be a critic, while inadequate as a qualitative judgment on one or both sides of her literary practice, does call attention to the deep-seated ambivalence toward critical agonism and, more broadly, toward all forms of negativity that Moore manifested throughout her writing career. In fact, Moore was at times not just ambivalent about the ugly feelings of agonism and negativity but openly antagonistic to them. As a subtly angry couplet in her 1923 poem "Marriage" has it: "Men have power / and sometimes one is made to feel it." Both of Moore's signature styles—her critical poetry and her poetic criticism—have their root in a single, complex desire: to avoid an overt posture of agonism, always associated in her mind with disagreeable masculinism, without sacrificing the critical agency associated with negative judgment. Moore wanted to wield critical and institutional influence without engaging in the agonistic public displays that Pound, Eliot, and other modernists savored; to have power, in other words, without taking up the cudgels.

◌◌◌ ◌◌◌ ◌◌◌

In July 1916, Moore published a poem titled "Critics and Connoisseurs" in *Others*, a little magazine published out of Grantwood, New Jersey. The editorial ethos of *Others* was bohemian and progressive, seeking to cultivate a generalized opposition to the American status quo more than promotion of any one aesthetic tendency. The *Others* writers "defined themselves as outsiders," as Suzanne Churchill put it, and maintained a basically agonistic stance not only toward the existing American literary culture but also toward society in general.[11] In this radical context, "Critics and Connoisseurs" strikes a rather equivocal note:

There is a great amount of poetry in unconscious
fastidiousness. Certain Ming
         products, imperial floor coverings of coach
wheel yellow, are well enough in their way but I have
                              seen something

         that I like better—a

mere childish attempt to make an imperfectly
            ballasted animal stand up,
      similar determination to make a pup
          eat his meat on the plate.

I remember a swan under the willows in Oxford
    with flamingo colored, maple-
          leaflike feet. It reconnoitered like a battle
ship. Disbelief and conscious fastidiousness were the staple
      ingredients in its
             disinclination to move. Finally its hardihood
                    was not proof against its
             proclivity to more fully appraise such bits
           of food as the stream

bore counter to it; it made away with what I gave it
    to eat. I have seen this swan and
        I have seen you; I have seen ambition without
understanding in a variety of forms. Happening to stand
        by an ant hill, I have
             seen a fastidious ant carrying a
           stick, north,
                   south, east, west,
                      till it turned on
          itself, struck out from the flower
          bed into the lawn,
             and returned to the point

from which it had started. Then abandoning the stick as
    useless and overtaxing its
        jaws, with a particle of whitewash pill-like but
heavy, it again went through the same course of procedure.
    What is
        there in being able
            to say that one has dominated the
          stream in an
                 attitude of
                 self-defense,

in proving that one has had the
experience
of carrying a stick?[12]

"Critics and Connoisseurs," while formally experimental enough
to consort well with the rest of the material included in *Others*, is a
very strange match for the magazine in its tone.[13] While the contributors to *Others* typically took provocatively agonistic stances
toward "traditional" American culture, the speaker of "Critics and
Connoisseurs" is at best ambivalent about all such stances. The
poem is a little fable about criticism and a meditation on two different ways of experiencing an artwork, ways that are allegorically
associated with the critic and the connoisseur, or the swan and the
ant, respectively. At the same time as the poem exhibits Moore's
typical fascination with agonistic criticism, there is a sense that the
speaker fundamentally distrusts the motives of those who "dominate . . . the stream in an/attitude of self-defense," like the Oxford
swan she describes (and who I argue represents the critic as opposed
to the connoisseur). The swan, despite its confidence and elegance,
is ultimately mercenary and self-interested: presented with a piece
of food, it gives up its strategic position and cynically "[makes] away
with what I gave it to eat."

Nothing could be further from this extravagant display of agonism than the actions of the humble ant, associated throughout
with the connoisseur. Where the swan acts strategically, the ant
goes unthinkingly through the motions, following a "course of procedure." Moore's admiration for hard work is well known, and it is
hard to read her evocation of the ant's pointless industriousness as
anything but sympathetic. Although its mindless ritual is also, in
the final analysis, a form of "ambition without understanding," Moore
greatly prefers it to the swan's crafty "reconnoiter[ing]."

So there is a significant distinction here between the critic and
the connoisseur, despite their common trait of "ambition without
understanding," which has eluded some of Moore's best commentators. The critic is consciously fastidious (like the swan dominating
the stream in an attitude of self-defense), while the connoisseur is
unconsciously fastidious (like the ant carrying the stick to no ap-

parent purpose). The swan / critic, in other words, corresponds closely to the disagreeable figures in Moore's barbed early poems, while the ant / connoisseur, while bearing a close similarity to the critic, is closer to the oblique self-portraits of her later animal poems (like "The Pangolin" or "Elephants"). Both are examples of "ambition without understanding," but there is only one of these "forms" that Moore herself wants to wholly disclaim: the aggressive, reconnoitering critic.

One might say, then, that Moore is associating herself with the lesser of two evils here, pledging allegiance to the unconsciously fastidious, habitually discerning practice of the connoisseur rather than the consciously fastidious, purposive activity of the critic. (The perfect attitude toward art would presumably be held by the artist or poet, a role the unfailingly self-diminishing Moore is unwilling to claim for herself, even under cover of allegory.) And we already know the answer to the poem's final rhetorical question— "What is / there in being able / to say that one has dominated the stream in an / attitude of self-defense, / in proving that one has had the experience / of carrying a stick?"—by virtue of the way it echoes the first line of the poem: "there is a great amount of poetry in" such things. Moore is, in effect, claiming even these agonistic critical habits, along with more congenial connoisseurship, for the cause of "poetry," or "the poet," while at the same time making a clear distinction: these habits are not themselves "poetry," although there is "a great amount of poetry" in them.

But the other, more idiomatic meaning of "what is there in it" also asserts itself in the poem's final sentence: that is, "What's the point of it?" Here Moore's essential skepticism about the public assertion of aesthetic judgment reemerges, and there is a final subtlety in the poem's argument that, again, has gone unnoticed by most commentators. My contention is that the entire final sentence of the poem describes only the critic's attitude, even though it borrows from the imagery previously used in connection with the connoisseur ("carrying a stick"). In other words, "proving one has had the experience" is what the critic, not the connoisseur, does. Critics not only have aesthetic experiences but must also work to prove that they've had them, whereas connoisseurs simply have, and cultivate having, such experiences, to no purposive end and with no desire for a posteriori justification or demonstration. (We've arrived, again, at Eliot's worry over the ephemerality of mere sensitivity: the lack of any permanent consequence of the aesthetic experience.) Although it may seem that Moore is keeping up the symmetry between swan and ant of the previous passages, she is in fact emphasizing a fundamental asymmetry in the comparison. In practice, both critics and connoisseurs approach works of art in the same way (ambitiously, without understanding), but only the critic feels the need to provide proofs of aesthetic understanding after the fact.

All these strict conceptual tensions are very elegantly resolved within the parameters of "Critics and Connoisseurs" itself; like all allegories, it has a satisfying finality to it once it is deciphered. But what Moore could reconcile in her art continued to be a source of tension in her life, and this connoisseurial solution to the problem of agonism raised serious problems for her with regard to the burgeoning culture of modernist criticism. For what social function can a mere connoisseur—who is firmly committed to art but not necessarily to reasoning about art, and certainly not to arguing about it—have in an exchange-based cultural economy built largely on agonistic public criticism? By eschewing an aggressive critical stance, Moore risked forfeiting her place in the modernist public sphere entirely, consigning herself to the same hinterland of sensibility to which Eliot would soon banish the likes of Symons and Swinburne.

However much she disapproved of their strikes and maneuvers and their battleship-like reconnoitering, Moore must have seen that the adversarial stances of writers like Eliot, Pound, and Williams and little magazines like *Others* facilitated sociability and solidarity among modernist writers. Moore could not participate in this agonistic social mode to the same extent as her peers. Beyond her personal ethical reservations, there were other obstacles to her assumption of the mantle of the public poet-critic: her gender and her Presbyterian religious background made it difficult for her to be as comfortably aggressive as some of her male peers. Yet to abjure any relation to the new society of modernist poet-critics that was being formed, in large part, through agonistic debate and mutual self-criticism would have been disastrous for Moore as a relative new-comer to that world. Her solution was to maintain a crucial relation to these arguments and interactions, but not an agonistic or "crit-ical" one: that of magazine editor.

∽∾ ∽∾ ∽∾

When Moore finally began to get involved in the editorial side of a little magazine in the early 1920s, it was not *Others*, which had been publishing her work consistently for years, but a periodical at once much more powerful and much closer to her aesthetic: the *Dial*. Although *Others* offered free rein to her experimental tendencies, Alfred Kreymborg's magazine was far more adversarial in tone than Moore desired to be. Given this situation, it is not at all surprising that in the early 1920s Moore began to move away from *Others* and toward the *Dial* as a more appropriate forum for her work. Recently acquired by Scofield Thayer and James Sibley Watson, the *Dial* was in the process of sloughing off its old identity as a progressive political organ (from 1918 to 1921 it printed John Dewey, Thorstein Veblen, Randolph Bourne, and Lewis Mumford) and refashioning itself as America's premier journal of "pure" art and literature.[14] If *Others* tended toward the agonistic, the *Dial* was devoutly pluralistic; in-deed, as historian Nicholas Joost put it, "Its pluralism . . . occasion-ally seemed to amount to indifference to the values of opposing ideas."[15] Put simply, the magazine refused to take decisive positions in matters of aesthetics or politics, much less to defend such posi-tions or elaborate them at length. (A reasonable twenty-first-century analogue might be the *Paris Review*.) For this reason, the new *Dial* was immediately mistrusted by two sets of important potential al-lies: on the one hand, political progressives like Mumford and Dewey who would have liked to see it take a more definite ideolog-ical stance; and on the other, representatives of the artistic and literary avant-garde who disliked its lack of critical policy and its hospitality to premodernist literature. But despite critiques of this kind, catholicity of taste continued to be the *Dial*'s modus operandi, a fact it proudly proclaimed in "Announcement" in June 1925: "We did not, and do not, deem that it is feasible, in aesthetic matters, to judge by reference to any detailed theoretic code."[16] The *Dial*'s resistance to theory, at least as a determining influence on aesthetic judgment, was implacable.

Reconstruction of this social context can help account for the intriguing defensiveness of Moore's poems from the early 1920s. Moore was in transition during this period from an early interest in women's suffrage and progressive politics to a more explicitly aestheticist phase (and, ultimately, a more conservative political position as well). In this, she was certainly in tune with Thayer and Watson's editorial policy, which eschewed political side taking in favor of the promotion of "interest" and "beauty." It is especially appropriate, then, that Moore's first appearance in the *Dial* in April 1920 was with "Picking and Choosing," a poem that imagines aesthetic judgment as an act of private selection rather than public contention:

> Literature is a phase of life: if
> > one is afraid of it, the situation is irremediable; if
> one approaches it familiarly,
> > what one says of it is worthless. Words are constructive
> when they are true; the opaque allusion—the simulated flight
>
> upward—accomplishes nothing. Why cloud the fact
> > that Shaw is selfconscious in the field of sentiment but
> > > is otherwise re-
> warding? that James is all that has been
> > said of him, if *feeling* is profound? It is not Hardy
> the distinguished novelist and Hardy the poet, but one man
>
> "interpreting life through the medium of the
> > emotions." If he must give an opinion, it is permissible
> > > that the
> critic should know what he likes. Gordon
> > Craig with his "this is I" and "this is mine," with his
> > > three
> wise men, his "sad French greens" and his Chinese cherries—
> > Gordon Craig, so
> inclinational and unashamed—has carried
> > the precept of being a good critic, to the last extreme;
> > > and Burke is a

psychologist—of acute, raccoon-
      like curiosity. *Summa diligentia;*
to the humbug, whose name is so amusing—very young and ve-

ry rushed, Caesar crossed the Alps on the "top of a
      diligence." We are not daft about the meaning but this
         familiarity
with wrong meanings puzzles one. Humming-
      bug, the candles are not wired for electricity.
Small dog, going over the lawn, nipping the linen and saying

that you have a badger—remember Xenophon;
      only the most rudimentary sort of behaviour is
         necessary
to put us on the scent; a "right good
      salvo of barks," a few "strong wrinkles" puckering the
skin between the ears, are all we ask.[17]

"Picking and Choosing," while posing as a statement of general principle, can also be read as a kind of manifesto for the *Dial*'s specific form of aesthetic connoisseurship. Although it was published five years before she took over the mantle of managing editor, it can be read as a proleptic statement of purpose for Moore's subsequent editorial activities there, or even as an early audition for the job. Moore is writing not just about her own subjective preferences or the normal process of selection necessarily involved in writing criticism, but about the kind of "picking and choosing" that go into putting together a magazine. In such instances, pluralism and aestheticism are not marks of sentimental vagueness but of practical savoir faire; what would normally be dismissed as signs of (feminine) weakness become crucial to the exercise of power.

Regarding the poem from this angle, one sees more readily why the editor of a prominent and closely scrutinized little magazine might be "afraid" of literature or resist "approach[ing] it familiarly"—that is, with preconceptions or favoritism. The maxim "Words are constructive when they are true," similarly, has a different resonance when it is applied to a rejection note than to a critical statement. At the same time at which Moore reserves the right to judge negatively, however, she is also marking the distance between the *Dial*'s ideal of criticism and the more agonistic mode favored by Pound, Eliot, and the *Others* group. Against these men and their brand of vigorous public critique, Moore posits the idiosyncratic British theater designer and critic Gordon Craig, who "has carried/the precept of being a good critic, to the last extreme." Here Moore appears to be advocating a subjective, evaluative, "inclinational and unashamed" criticism over a more objective, analytical one: "If he must give an opinion, it is permissible that the/critic should know what he likes."

"Picking and Choosing" concludes with the speaker's proud refusal to justify or rationalize her subjective aesthetic judgments. Judgments of taste are, for Moore, simply not the sorts of things that one can reasonably account for, nor should one waste one's time trying. They are, instead, instinctive and irrational, belonging to the animal rather than the human order of intelligence: and she, the all-powerful editor of the *Dial*, is, on the aesthetic level, analogous to the "small dog" who exhibits a "rudimentary" but nonetheless adequate sense of interest and value. The business of criticism, for Moore, is not fundamentally about contentions, which are public and open to challenge, but about choices, which are private and not in need of external justification. When one is picking and choosing, there's no need to explain oneself.

❧❧❧

The story of Moore's career trajectory over the course of the 1920s is one of ascension to institutional power: her reputation was, for many years, inseparable from the reputation of the *Dial*. Certainly her contemporaries regarded her, sometimes angrily or enviously, as powerful. But Moore's power, like Eliot's, required a patron. Scofield Thayer had the most direct impact on Moore's personal and professional circumstances and was in many ways the crucial figure for understanding Moore's early development. The heir to a Massachusetts wool-mill fortune and a Harvard contemporary of E. E. Cummings and T. S. Eliot, Thayer went in a short time from being a contributor to the *Dial* to being an investor and then a co-owner (with James Sibley Watson), editor, and publisher. As impresario of the *Dial*, he was largely responsible for initiating and overseeing the changes to the magazine's aesthetic policy discussed in the previous section. In addition to his literary interests, Thayer was also a prolific collector of modern art, and he had a particularly strong influence on the selection of visual art reproduced in the magazine.[18] It was at Thayer's behest that the *Dial* began publishing Moore's work in 1921, and he quickly became her most vocal champion, praising her work in his editorial comments and granting her the *Dial* award for 1924.

All of this makes Thayer is an obvious figure to consider in connection with Moore's 1921 poem "When I Buy Pictures," which, like "Picking and Choosing," is subtly but significantly transformed by reading it in the context of her professional association with the *Dial*. I include the title here since, as is often the case with Moore, it forms part of the poem:

When I Buy Pictures

Or what is closer to the truth,
when I look at that of which I may regard myself as the
    imaginary possessor,
I fix upon what would give me pleasure in my average
    moments:
the satire upon curiosity in which no more is discernible than
the intensity of the mood;
or quite the opposite—the old thing, the mediaeval decorated
    hat-box,
in which there are hounds with waists diminishing like the
    waist of the hourglass
and deer and birds and seated people;
it may be no more than a square of parquetry; the literal
    biography perhaps,
in letters standing well apart upon a parchment-like expanse;
an artichoke in six varieties of blue; the snipe-legged
    hieroglyphic in three parts;
the silver fence protecting Adam's grave, or Michael taking
    Adam by the wrist.
Too stern an intellectual emphasis upon this quality or that,
    detracts from one's enjoyment;

it must not wish to disarm anything; nor may the approved
   triumph easily be honored—
that which is great because something else is small.
It comes to this: of whatever sort it is,
it must be "lit with piercing glances into the life of things";
it must acknowledge the spiritual forces which have made it.[19]

The use of the first person, relatively rare in Moore's poetry, in the first three lines invites us to read "When I Buy Pictures" as a dramatic monologue. But who is speaking—and potentially buying—here? The first-person speaker implied by the title encourages us to read it as a kind of confessional poem issuing from Moore's own subject position, but this "I" makes more sense from the mouth of a wealthy art collector like Thayer than it does from a petit bourgeois poet-critic like Moore, who could not often afford to purchase expensive works of art for herself. (Most of the art objects in her home, even in later years, were gifts from more prosperous friends rather than personal acquisitions.) Is it Scofield Thayer, then—a rich and powerful patron of the arts—who is speaking? Or Moore, his factotum? The poem seems to swerve between a total identification with Thayer (in which case it is indeed he, or someone like him, who is speaking here) and a partial one (in which case it is Moore, or someone like her, speaking on behalf of her employer). Look again at the poem's first lines, which run continuously on from the title's syntax:

Or what is closer to the truth,
when I look at that of which I may regard myself as the imaginary
   possessor,
I fix upon what would give me pleasure in my average moments.

The first line is a typically Mooresque self-correction: the speaker is immediately concerned to get "closer to the truth" than the title "When I Buy Pictures" has already brought her. The "truth" is that Moore is not Thayer, a wealthy connoisseur who purchases things purely for the sake of his own pleasure; she is an impoverished art lover who can afford only to be the "imaginary possessor" of expensive artworks. Thus the "I" represents both Moore herself and the person she would like to be, namely, Thayer. The patron is a kind of second self, a version of the poet-critic who not only makes well-founded judgments of taste but also has the economic power to act on them.[20]

In 1921, four years before she would assume her official duties at the *Dial*, this was nothing but a slightly embarrassed fantasy: Moore imagines herself as the buyer she couldn't become, and she goes on to give a fanciful list of features she would use as criteria for her purchases if she could. What follows this highly qualified opening clause is a list, characteristic of Moore's poetry in this period, of aesthetic qualities and features that she found pleasing in various works of art: "It may be no more than a square of parquetry . . . an artichoke in six varieties of blue; the snipe-legged hieroglyphic in three parts," and so on. This litany of impressions and observations concludes with an anticritical mission statement that has something of the tone of "Picking and Choosing":

> Too stern an intellectual emphasis upon this quality or that,
>   detracts from one's enjoyment;
> it must not wish to disarm anything; nor may the approved
>   triumph easily be honored—that
>   which is great because something else is small.

Just as in "Picking and Choosing" Moore dismissed critical explications and rationalizations as overzealous "humbug," here she comes out against "too stern an intellectual emphasis on this quality or that," thus undermining even the descriptive and comparative methods of criticism along with its claim to a rational basis. In contrast to the earlier poem, however, her anticritical stance in "When I Buy Pictures" doesn't oppose a different, purer type of criticism, "inclinational and unashamed," to intellectualist theorization. Instead, she opposes something else to criticism of both kinds, imagining herself not as a critic or connoisseur but as a different kind of social actor entirely: a consumer. Where, in "Picking and Choosing," the "inclinational and unashamed" critic could dispense with the exhausting theoretical justifications of the psychologist, now the discerning buyer can dispense even with the apparatus of criticism. In matters of commerce, taste is all: *de gustibus non est disputandum*.

Moore's 1925 appointment as managing editor of the *Dial* made the scenario described in "When I Buy Pictures" into a reality. As Thayer's employee, Moore was in a certain sense "buying" material, but not in order to take possession of it herself. Acting as managing editor thus allowed her to indulge her tastes and desires as the connoisseur would, but without any of the guilt of personal satisfaction to trouble her scrupulous Protestant conscience. After all, she was not just buying things on behalf of herself—although the aesthetic judgments behind the purchases were hers and hers alone—but disinterestedly, on behalf of a cultural institution (the *Dial*) and a grateful public (its readers). Thus she was able to preemptively deflect some of the adverse personal criticism that she feared might be directed at her, either for her self-indulgence or even, possibly, her deficits of taste. Similarly, the humble appeal to "what would give me pleasure in my average moments" suggests not an aesthetic extravagance but an almost ascetic labor of self-denial or public service, an attempt to judge fairly based on what was "average" in her own subjectivity: "It's not for me; it's for them."

The sense of epiphany and celebration in this rather joyous poem is linked to Moore's midlife discovery of her true métier: that of poet-editor, a role that resolves the tasks of critic and connoisseur into a single function. Certainly this is one way to read its closing lines:

> It comes to this: of whatever sort it is,
>   it must be "lit with piercing glances into the life of
>   things";
>   it must acknowledge the spiritual forces
>   which have made it.

The frank, decisive "It comes to this"—so atypical of the circumlocutionary Moore—is not merely the subjective judgment of a critic or a connoisseur. Rather, it is the bottom line as laid down by a practical social actor, such as a magazine editor. It appears as if Moore had finally resolved the great problem of her early career—how to express her own strong preferences and judgments in a way that involved her in the society of modernism without engaging in acts of aggression or critical agonism—and indeed, for all intents and purposes, she had. No longer a direct competitor of other poet-critics, she established herself as a gatekeeper whom those poet-critics had to pass in order to gain entry to the modernist public sphere. Thus, by "picking and choosing" and, furthermore, buying and acting as an "imaginary possessor," Moore was able to make herself indispensable to the society of literary modernism without accepting the uncongenial role of the agonistic poet-critic. This was no small accomplishment, and we should not be surprised that a certain self-satisfaction attends it. In the world in which Moore made a place for herself, editors have power, and sometimes critics are made to feel it.

3

Student Bodies

ALTHOUGH T. S. ELIOT would provide the most influential model for the institutional, and especially the academic, poet-critic, he himself remained cautious about his institutional affiliations. As early as 1920, the year of *The Sacred Wood*'s publication, I. A. Richards tried to secure Eliot for the faculty of the fledgling English School at Cambridge. "I was . . . full of dreams of somehow winkling Eliot out of his bank and annexing him to Cambridge," Richards remembered in 1965.[1] Eliot, however, was wary of being annexed to a university. Although he had more of an academic background than any of his fellow modernists, he clearly preferred to preserve his extramural status with regard to academia, resisting incorporation into the institution without severing contact entirely.

In retrospect, this was surely wise. As an academic in the 1920s, Eliot would have been at best a curiosity. Moreover, he would have been, as Richards put it, "annexed" to an institutional project that was not his own: the legitimation of English studies as an academic discipline grounded in theoretical concepts borrowed from psychology and analytic philosophy. As editor of the *Criterion*, in contrast, Eliot would be setting the intellectual agenda. It is quite possible that the idea for such a journal was already in his mind by the time Richards approached him about the Cambridge position; in any case, starting a magazine was entirely consistent with Eliot's focus on the journalistic rather than the academic field, as demonstrated in Chapter 1.

Along with F. R. Leavis's *Scrutiny* (based in Cambridge) and a handful of other little magazines, Eliot's *Criterion* was a major venue for the writers of what would become known as the Auden Generation. This was a generation whose members were learning to be poet-critics at a time when the social roles and practices of the critic were changing dramatically. There was a political element at work in this: the Auden Generation was, famously, a left-leaning generation, many of whose members embraced communism and wrote on specifically political topics, and this leftward turn gave the idea of "criticism," as we will see later, a decidedly new ideological valence. For the most part, however, the increasing emphasis on criticism in the 1930s was just a further elaboration of the transformation of the social role of the poet-critic that writers like Pound, Eliot, and Moore had already ushered in. Although they wrote a different kind of criticism from the high modernists, taking different political positions and aiming at different kinds of rhetorical effects, it is indisputable that the type of the English poet-critic in the 1930s owed an enormous debt to the first generation of modernist poet-critics, and to Eliot in particular.

Louis Menand has proposed that "Eliot owed his success as a cultural figure in England in part to his arriving precisely at the moment when one style of critical discourse was yielding in importance and authority to another." For him, Eliot's rise is one indicator of a larger historical shift in the culture of English literary criticism: "The sort of freelance, journal-based literary criticism practiced by the members of the Bloomsbury group was being displaced by a new, university-based type: the criticism of the academic with an interest in the condition of contemporary culture."[2] Menand is not wrong, but, like many historians of modernism, he rushes too quickly to where we all know things ended up: "university-based . . . criticism," heavily indebted to Eliot and his fellow modernists but circulating within a very different textual economy. Here I propose that we dwell a little longer on the precarious institutional arrangement of the early 1920s, before Eliot's reputation was made outside a few networks of precocious student intellectuals. Before the power of modernism became invested in English departments and administrations, it resided within student bodies in a dual sense: specific undergraduate populations but also in the bodies—the dispositions, tastes, preferences, elective affinities, and likes and dislikes—of the youths who made them up.

With these prewar social conditions in mind, I want to resist one easy narrative about what happened to Eliot and other modernist poet-critics between 1920 and 1950. This narrative casts them as brilliant amateurs, comfortably (or not so comfortably) ensconced in the world outside the university: denizens of bookstores, little magazines, salons, and other nonacademic environments who were suspicious of formal education and dry-as-dust scholarship. Certainly support can be found for this narrative: Pound (who earned a master's degree from the University of Pennsylvania in 1906) rarely failed to rail against the university system in both England and the United States; and even Eliot, that most donnish of modernists, sometimes struck anti-academic postures.

But the prewar situation is rather more complicated than that, even if one leaves aside the fact that all the major modernist poets were college educated, and that many of them (Pound, Eliot, Stein, Williams) even possessed graduate degrees. It only seems possible to tell the story of interwar modernism without the university; and it seems possible in part because modernist poet-critics so often disavowed or deemphasized their academic connections. But the fact remains that much crucial early support for modernist literature—not financial support but readers, that most fundamental resource for writers—did come from universities; it just didn't come from professors. In fact, it was university students who responded most avidly to modernism in its formative years.

Notably, it was not simply, or even primarily, modernist poetry or fiction that excited the undergraduates of the 1920s; it was modernist criticism. In his reminiscence of Eliot's influence at Oxford, the literary scholar F. W. Bateson recalled that "*The Sacred Wood* was almost our sacred book. It was Eliot the critic who prepared us to welcome Eliot the poet, and not vice versa."[3] James Reeves, in a similar memoir of Cambridge, echoed this religious language: "The stranger who enters an Anglican church at service time is handed two books, *Hymns Ancient and Modern* and *The Book of Common Prayer.* ... When I went up to Cambridge ... I was handed as it were, in much the same spirit, two little books, the one in prose, the other in verse. They were *The Sacred Wood* and *Poems 1909–1925*."[4]

By the mid-1920s, then, Eliot was a major figure among undergraduates at both Oxford and Cambridge. Although his vogue was broadly similar at both universities, it's worth distinguishing the two because their peculiar institutional characters inflected the quality of his influence slightly but significantly in both cases. The cult of Eliot at Cambridge was linked both to a broader interest in the metaphysical and Elizabethan poets (groups well represented and reevaluated in *The Sacred Wood*) and to a rebellious aestheticism that had not yet been channeled, as it would be throughout the 1930s, into radical political activity. (James Reeves, who was at Cambridge in the early 1920s, called his cohort "the last generation of [Cambridge] undergraduates to remain more or less indifferent to politics.")[5] To the student literary crowd at Cambridge in the early to mid-1920s, Eliot was a formative influence.[6] William Empson, who, along with Auden, would become the most significant English poet-critic of his generation, wrote, in his 1948 memoir "The Style of the Master," that "I feel . . . I do not know how much of my own mind he invented, let alone how much of it is a reaction against him or indeed a consequence of misreading him. He has a very penetrating influence, perhaps not unlike an east wind."[7] Similarly, the poet Kathleen Raine, a contemporary of Empson's who would go on to become an accomplished poet and scholar, claimed that Eliot's "work forms, for my generation, so much a part of what for us is the permanent reality of the world."[8]

At Oxford, the cult of Eliot was, if anything, even more extreme. He had briefly been a scholar there, doing graduate work in philosophy at Merton College from 1914 to 1915 (an experience he disliked profoundly; "In Oxford," he wrote to Conrad Aiken that year, "I have the feeling that I am not quite alive—that my body is walking about with a bit of my brain inside it, and nothing else. . . . Oxford is very pretty, but I don't like to be dead").[9] Unlike in Cambridge, where the reigning commitments to rationalism and secular liberalism made much of his emerging conservative Christian ideology a tough sell, there was extensive overlap between Eliot's critical doctrines and the official philosophies of Oxford humanism: for instance, the high value placed on the classics and an Arnoldian concern for cultural and social reform. But ideological affinities alone can't explain the snug fit between Eliot and the Oxford undergraduates of the late 1920s. Certainly they can't account for the fact that Eliot's work was frequently taken up, as we shall see, by students as a symbol of revolt against the academic institution and its values.

To understand this phenomenon, we need to look instead at more material factors. For one thing, Oxford's geographic proximity to London allowed its students easy access to Eliot, and vice versa. Although the fellows of All Souls College denied his 1926 application for a research fellowship, he nonetheless made his presence felt by speaking to undergraduate societies such as the Martlets.[10] Unsurprisingly, then, memoirs of Eliot by poets who attended Oxford in the 1920s tend to speak less of his "influence" than of his "presence." Stephen Spender, for instance, wrote in a 1966 Festschrift for Eliot that "to our generation, Eliot was the poet of poets, closer to us than Yeats though Yeats might be 'greater.'"[11] By "closer to us" Spender means both more accessible in subject matter and physically closer: "*The Waste Land* was exciting . . . because it was concerned with the life which we felt to be real. . . . The poet . . . had the sense of our problems. . . . 'The young man carbuncular' who assaulted 'The typist home at teatime' had a great deal in common with any undergraduate who went down to London and had a whore in a bed-sitting room, returning, in time to climb into college, by the train called 'the fornicator.'"[12]

But Eliot's "closeness" and "presence" to young Oxonians are a matter not only of the aesthetic or thematic qualities of his work or of his geographic proximity but also of his temperamental hospitality toward younger writers. Spender continues:

> The secret of Eliot's influence over the young lay in a paradox of his personality. . . . The man who seemed so unapproachable was the most approached by the younger poets—and the most helpful to them—of any poet of his generation. Whoever had the will and intelligence to do so could grasp the principles by which he worked and lived, could read what he had read, could

understand what he believed. All this was far more important than whether one agreed with all his opinions. One could see the relevance of his relation to the time in which he lived, and to the past. Religiously, poetically, and intellectually, this very private man kept open house. And all the rooms, and the garden, made clear sense.[13]

This emphasis on the importance of Eliot's personality may seem surprising, even irreverent, given his famous theoretical commitment to the impersonal. But this is exactly why Eliot appeared so attractive to Oxford undergraduates of the 1920s: even as he campaigned in print against the Romantic mystique of the poet as "personality," he was personally available to them in a way in which few other major writers were. For Oxford student poets, Eliot became a kind of local oracle, like the Cumaean Sibyl from the epigraph to *The Waste Land*. But unlike more purely vatic mentor figures like Arthur Symons or W. B. Yeats or even Pound, Eliot was rational, reasonable. His beliefs were unfamiliar but, with a little labor, comprehensible: "All the rooms, and the garden, made clear sense."

༺ ༻ ༺ ༻ ༺ ༻

One of the young Oxford poets whom Eliot and the *Criterion* supported was W. H. Auden. Auden first rose to prominence among his schoolmates as a wunderkind, the poet-critic most likely to succeed. He coedited two consecutive editions of the annual *Oxford Poetry* anthology, and his earliest published works, like *Paid on Both Sides: A Charade*, deliberately exploit the cloistered ambiance of the university and the public school, as if encouraging readers' identification of him with elite education. (Hardly any of the early reviews of his poetry fail to mention his Oxford connection.)

Yet by the time Auden published his first long poem, *The Orators*, in 1932, he had begun to feel a sort of anxiety about his institutional pedigree, especially as he and the rest of his cohort drifted toward communism. Both the left and the right were increasingly seeing Oxbridge and the public schools as synonymous with a British class system on the verge of imminent collapse. Many of Auden's early critical pieces were reviews not of poetry or other literary works but of nonfiction books on education, and these indicate his increasing pessimism about the future of the British school system as it was currently constituted, as well as his own professional role within it. "Like everything else in our civilisation, the system we have made has become too much for us," he writes in "Private Pleasure," a review of three books on education for *Scrutiny* in September 1932. "All we can do is become specialists. Just as the soldier devises new methods of gas attack, or the poet a new technique of verbal association, the teacher vigorously pursues the logic of his tiny department. . . . No one can afford to stop and ask what is the bearing of his work on the rest of the world, its ultimate value. It's his job, his bread and butter."[14] Even more pointed is this remark in an October 1932 review of Bertrand Russell's *Education and the Social Order:* "The failure of modern education lies not in its attention to individual needs, nor to methods, nor even to the moral ideas it preaches, but in the fact that nobody genuinely believes in our society, for which the children are being trained."[15] In 1934 he contributed an essay bearing the provocative title "The Liberal Fascist" to *The Old School*, a collection of essays on public-school education edited by Graham Greene, which culminates in a calculatedly incendiary comparison: "The best reason I have for opposing Fascism is that at school I lived in a Fascist state."[16]

Yet although the Auden of the early 1930s found much to criticize in the English educational system, he also returns to it again and again as a model of communal life, and his poetry and his criticism alike are characterized by a persistent anxiety about the prospect of being expelled from it. Although he tried hard to cloak his concern with education in the mantle of radical politics, it also had to do with a more practical question of authorial self-presentation. Should he repudiate his educational privilege, or should he trade on it? Was being an "Oxford poet" a tradition he wanted to uphold in a period of conspicuous progressivism and antielitism?

With *The Orators*, Auden made a bid to be seen as more than just an Oxford poet while still remaining careful to remind his readers that he was an Oxford poet. By deliberately steeping his most experimental writing in what one critic of the poem called "schoolboyish crudity" and "undergraduate cleverness," not to mention direct references to his educational experience, Auden was able to ruthlessly criticize the English school system while emphasizing his personal relation to it. His connection to Oxford and, more generally, to the public schools and the British elite educational system enabled *The Orators'* critique (since no one but an insider would know enough to make such criticisms), legitimized it (since no one else would be taken as seriously), and, in a sense, neutralized it (since no one who had so obviously benefited from the system could be seen as seriously militating against it). Indeed, the very status that allowed Auden to credibly criticize the school system—his participation in its social rituals and confident mastery of its codes—was also his chief claim to authority in the first place.

The opening of *The Orators* is very much concerned with how such rhetorical authority is attained. In October 1931 Auden published a short prose monologue in the *Criterion*, "Speech for a Prize-Day" (later lightly revised and retitled "Address for a Prize-Day"), the first section of his forthcoming long poem to see print. In or out of the context of *The Orators*, the text is somewhat mysterious. From the title and other internal evidence, we can confidently discern that its setting is a school, and that the speaker is addressing a student body, perhaps in an assembly setting. Beyond that, however, things are less clear, beginning with the age of the students and the exact level of the school system we are dealing with; as Stephen Burt has put it, school and university "in Auden's imagination . . . are continuous."[17] "Address for a Prize-Day," like much else in *The Orators*, seems to incorporate elements of preparatory school, public school, and university into one condensed institutional image, a sort of sociological dream work.

The "Address" is Auden's first extended exercise in parody: it mimics the mannerisms of Cyril Morgan-Brown, the headmaster at St. Edmund's, Auden's preparatory school. (Morgan-Brown was a stock impression of Auden's, according to Christopher Isherwood: "[He] was brilliant at doing one of Pa's sermons: how he wiped his glasses, how he coughed, how he clicked his fingers when somebody in chapel fell asleep ('Sn Edmund's Day . . . Sn Edmund's Day . . . Whur ders it *mean?* Nert—whur did it mean to *them, then, theah?* Bert—whur ders it mean to *ers, heah, nerw?*').")[18] But although the tics are borrowed from Morgan-Brown, the exact identity of the orator is ambiguous: some critical accounts have him as a headmaster, while others suggest that he is "an old boy down for the day"—that is, an alumnus returning to address the currently matriculating students.[19]

Whatever the speaker's identity, the most obvious rhetorical feature of his discourse is its slow, lugubrious, almost liturgical aspect: its rhythmic heaviness, empty repetitions, and ornamental commonplaces. "Commemoration. Commemoration. What does it mean? What does it mean?" he begins, with a series of dull thuds. "Not what does it mean to them, there, then. What does it mean to us, here, now?"[20] This opening is merely pro forma, it seems, since the rest of the speech is not really on the theme of commemoration at all; indeed, it is focused on the present and the future, not the past. (We might note that the word "commemoration" contains the word "oration" within it; thus this "commemoration," or "remembering together," is also a "communal oration.") In "Address for a Prize-Day," Auden imagines a kind of primal scene of British education: the moment when a collective sense of special destiny and duty is effectively transmitted to an elite group. When the orator enjoins his audience to "imagine to yourselves a picked body of angels, all qualified experts on the human heart, a Divine Commission, arriving suddenly one day at Dover," he is asking them not just to "imagine to [them]selves" but also, by implication, to imagine themselves as this heavenly "body." As privileged inheritors of the English humanist culture of feeling, the members of the orator's audience are indeed "qualified experts on the human heart"—or, at any rate, they have the potential, and now the desire, to become such. (The ambiguous age of the initiates—is this a prep school? a public school? a university?—also matters. If this is an audience of children, they are being asked to imagine the university men they will one day become.)

Having introduced the idea of this "picked body of angels," the orator goes on to describe their imminent dispersal: "After some weeks in London, they separate. . . . And then when every inch of the ground has been carefully gone over, every house inspected, they return to the Capital again to compare notes, to collaborate in a complete report, which made, they depart as quickly as they came."[21] These scenes of surveillance recall the "secret agent" imagery of Auden's first post-Oxford poems; he would continue to play with such iconography throughout the 1930s and even into the 1940s, as we shall see. But the image of communal dispersal also evokes the trajectories of Auden and his Oxford classmates, most of whom took up teaching posts at various schools around England soon after graduation; schoolmasters, too, are "qualified experts on the human heart." "Beauty of the scenery apart, would you not feel some anxiety as to the contents of that report?" the orator asks the initiates. "Do you consider their statistics as to the average number of lost persons to the acre would be a cause for self-congratulation? Take a look round this hall, for instance. What do you think? What do you think about England, this country of ours where nobody is well?" This unexpected reversal of the audience's attention, turning its concerned gaze back on itself ("Take a look round this hall"), transforms the description of the social world into a silent indictment of the elite minority who stand apart from it. Thus the orator's bleak picture of a nation "where nobody is well" functions as a call to the initiates to do something to cure or change it.

The central question of "Address for a Prize-Day" is not whether Auden is mocking or endorsing what the orator has to say. (As so often with the early Auden, he seems to be doing a little of both.) Instead, we should attend to how the orator manages to create in his hearers an anxious expectation about what will happen after this "picked body of angels" disperses and the temporary community of the school is no more. There is a strong suggestion, borne out by the rest of books 1 and 2 of *The Orators*, that it will be something sinister, for here Auden makes a sudden hairpin turn here from a parody of the language of the English public school and its ideals of liberal social reform to that of fascism, with its public denunciations and calls to violence: "You've got some pretty stiff changes to make. We simply can't afford any passengers or skrimshankers. I should like to see you make a beginning before I go, now, here. Draw up a list of rotters and slackers, of proscribed persons under headings like this. Committees for municipal or racial improvement—the headmaster. Disbelievers in the occult—the school chaplain. The bogusly cheerful—the games master. The really disgusted—the teacher of modern languages. All these have got to die without issue."[22]

This stark transition, in which expulsion from the student body is figured as a sort of social death, sets up the next few sections of *The Orators*, which explore fascist imagery in a cryptic modernist mode adapted from Eliot, D. H. Lawrence, St. John Perse, and others. *The Orators* has often been read as a poem about the temptations of political totalitarianism, whether right or left, fascist or Communist. Either the poem is a satire on totalitarianism, critics have argued, or it is an extended flirtation with it. Edward Mendelson, for instance, writes that "*The Orators* . . . is an account of everything a group ought not to be. . . . Auden began it as a deliberately negative vision of groups, but as he worked on it, and after he published it, he came to recognize that he had favored his negative vision more than he thought."[23] Such a reading is consonant with Auden's oft-quoted later assessment of *The Orators* as a "fair notion fatally injured," a critique of fascism that doubled as a dalliance with it; it seemed to have been written, he thought, by "someone talented but near the border of sanity, who might well, in a year or two, become a Nazi."[24]

But a critical focus on *The Orators*' ambivalent attitude toward totalitarianism places too much emphasis on the "Journal of an Airman" section and risks reducing Auden's very specific interest in education to a matter of metaphoric convenience. Education, not politics, is the real theme of *The Orators*. Furthermore, the focus on totalitarianism neglects the development of the poem's themes in book 3, where Auden moves beyond the paranoia that dominated the first two books and begins to consider seriously the question of the school as a formative community.

This development may have been prompted by Auden's newfound employment as an educator. In April 1930, after a couple of years of living in London and Berlin supported by his family, Auden took a job teaching English and French at Larchfield Academy in Helensburgh, Scotland. "Financial exigencies forced him to teach," his biographer Richard Davenport-Hines writes:

> The spoilt or captious behaviour of contemporaries who could afford not to take jobs but wasted their opportunities was exas-

perating to him. "As the one who has to have the job, *I* am naturally jealous of you and Christopher who can do as you please," he wrote to [Stephen] Spender . . . in 1933. "I don't think you know all the humiliations and exploitations of one's weakness that a job like mine involves, how hard it is to preserve any kind of integrity. If I ever sound complacent about it, it is because as compensation I exaggerate its occasional exquisite moments of satisfaction."[25]

Thus the 1930s inaugurated a new phase of Auden's already vexed relation to the British school system, but it also provided him with a new kind of poetic opportunity because the "occasional exquisite moments of satisfaction" that he was able to glean from his day job would form the basis of a new, more public poetics.

The final section of *The Orators*, "Six Odes," is often read, correctly, as marking the beginning of Auden's attempt to leave behind the obscurity of his earliest work and to find a more broadly accessible style. It is in the odes, too, that we see a definitive formal break with the aesthetic techniques of modernism that dominate the poem's earlier sections, because all the odes employ set forms established in the nineteenth century or earlier. This change in form, however, should not disguise the fact that Auden's preoccupations in the odes are much the same as they are in the earlier, more formally experimental sections.

It is significant, too, that this section, composed at Larchfield, returns to the theme of the school found in "Address for a Prize-Day," but it moves from the students' perspective to the teacher's, a shift in perspective that Auden registers by adopting the form of the Pindaric ode. Whereas the rhetorical address always posits some kind of audience that it is meant to persuade, the ode is most often directed at an object that cannot or will not reply and perhaps can't even hear in the usual sense. (Keats's "Ode on a Grecian Urn" is the classic example.) While "Address for a Prize Day" puts the reader in the same rhetorical position as the initiates, the odes regard the student body as a silent muse whose mute presence inspires the poet to song. The collective, nonindividuated aspect of the student body—the fact that it is not actually a single human body but a collection of many—is crucial here; Auden's move toward a more public style is accompanied by a newfound interest in community and solidarity.

The second ode—cut, probably for political as well as aesthetic reasons, from the later, revised edition of *The Orators*—is perhaps the clearest example of Auden's turn (or return) to traditional verse forms and on its face poses the fewest interpretive difficulties of any individual section of the poem. It is dedicated to Auden's Oxford friend Gabriel Carritt, "Captain of Sedbergh School XV." Although it was written in 1931, along with most of the rest of *The Orators*, it is dated "Spring, 1927" in order to commemorate a visit Auden made to Sedbergh after his graduation from Oxford, but before his subsequent employment as a schoolteacher. Davenport-Hines writes that Auden thought of Sedbergh as "in every respect his idea of 'paradise,'" a view that accounts for the rapturous quality of the ode.[26] The section thus has a nostalgic, even regressive quality: in its subject matter as well as its form, it represents a return to a position and attitude the poet had previously abandoned. The poem, a Pindaric ode written in diction that owes much to Gerard Manley Hopkins, describes a football match in terms that border on the ecstatic. In contrast to the strenuously prosaic aesthetic of books 1 and 2, there is a burst of exuberant lyricism:

> Walk on air do we? And how!
> With the panther's pad, with his lightness
> Never did members conspire till now
> > In such whole gladness:
> Currents of joy incalculable in ohms
> Wind from the spine along the moving arms
Over the great alkali wastes of the bowel, calming them too.[27]

The thrill running through the student body here is quasi-orgasmic (or possibly, given the presence of "air," "wind" and "the bowel," flatulent, a characteristically juvenile touch). As almost always in *The Orators*, there is a distancing irony in the presentation of this pleasure: the rhetorical question and answer ("Walk on air do we? And how!") seem deliberately awkward, for instance, and the "currents of joy incalculable . . . in ohms" (a measurement of electrical current) rather too technically specific (some of these kids must be studying engineering). Yet the second ode quite literally fetishizes the student body, fondly anatomizing its parts, its "members," "spine," "arms," and "bowel."

Although the poet's tongue is most certainly lodged in his cheek, the second ode should not be read simply as a satire on school athletics. Rather, it celebrates the fact that school life can be experienced in this way, that it can offer a real sense of community to its students, at least for a while. The divide between this utopian vision of school life and Auden's own more muted experience, both as student and teacher, accounts for the tonal ambiguity of this poem: the speaker's studied distance from the students' "currents of joy"—a "current" joy, as opposed to his own, presumably retrospective happiness— "incalculable in ohms" suggests a scientific relation to a natural phenomenon. In later stanzas, too, Auden deliberately courted cliché ("Standing up, waving, cheering from car, / The time of their life: / The fags are flushed, would die at their heroes' feet") in order to preserve ironic detachment while also suggesting an innocent pastoral enjoyment. The schoolboys of Sedbergh seek no fresher expressions than "the time of their life" or "would die at their . . . feet," and this is exactly what the poet wishes to celebrate about them.

The evocation of this jocular schoolboy atmosphere, which is without precedent in *The Orators* or in any of Auden's published poetry up to that point, makes possible a shift in tone in what is perhaps the most significant passage in the ode:

> Heart of the heartless world
> Whose pulse we count upon;
> Alive, the live [*sic*] on which you have called
> > Both pro and con,
> Good to a gillie, to an elver times out of mind
> Tender, to work-shy and game-shy kind
> Does he think? Not as kind as all that; he shall find one fine
> day he is sold.[28]

The first line of this stanza, as Mendelson and many others have pointed out, is an obvious allusion to Karl Marx's famous pronouncement on religion from the introduction to his *Critique of Hegel's Philosophy of Right*: "Religious distress is at the same time the expression of real distress and the protest against real distress. Religion is the sigh of the oppressed creature, the heart of a heartless world, just as it is the spirit of a spiritless situation. It is the opium of the people."[29]

Marx's unexpected appearance on the rugby field serves a number of functions. First, it is an oblique comment on the irony of a political radical like Gabriel Carritt—who by 1931 was an official member of the Communist Party—presiding over such wholesome play.[30] But the allusion also evokes the larger context of Marx's essay, which is largely concerned not with religion as such but with the role of philosophical criticism (*Kritik*) in bringing about historical change. Although Marx regards "the critique of religion [as] the prerequisite of every critique," he is not satisfied to let philosophy's efforts end there: "It is above all the task of philosophy, which is in the service of history, to unmask human self-alienation in its secular forms, once its sacred form has been unmasked. Thus, the critique of heaven is transformed into the critique of the earth, the critique of religion into the critique of law, the critique of theology into the critique of politics."[31] Critique, for Marx, is not free to choose what it opposes and what it considers acceptable; it has, rather, to transform the world by extending itself to every sphere. The conditions of contemporary life oblige philosophical critics to attack not only worthy opponents but unworthy ones as well, even those who are "beneath the level of history, beneath all criticism," who

> remain an object of criticism just as the criminal who is beneath the level of humanity remains an object of the executioner. In its struggle against them criticism is no passion of the brain, but is rather the brain of passion. It is not a scalpel but a weapon. Its object is its enemy, which it wishes not to refute but to destroy. For the spirit of these conditions is already refuted. They are not, in themselves, objects worthy of thought, but rather existences equally despicable and despised. Criticism itself needs no further self-clarification regarding this object, for criticism already understands it. Criticism is no longer an end in itself, but now simply a means.[32]

Whether Auden read Marx's whole text or simply knew the slogan "Heart of a heartless world," it is likely that he was familiar with this radicalized notion of *Kritik* from his Communist friends and would have associated it more or less directly with Marxism. (The emphasis would soon be made, in any case, by Marxist literary critics like Christopher Caudwell and Alick West, whose *Crisis and Criticism* appeared in 1937.) For Marx, "criticism" was no longer taken to be an "end in itself," an activity conducted on the purely intellectual plane of reason; it was "simply a means," less a diagnostic than a destructive practice, "not a scalpel but a weapon." Confronting his own "country where nobody is well" in the 1840s, Marx insists that social criticism must be "criticism in hand-to-hand combat; and in this kind of combat one does not bother about whether the opponent is noble, or of equal rank, or interesting; all that matters is to strike him." The passage's final sentence could serve as a summation of Auden's poetry and criticism in the 1930s, which constantly shuttles back and forth between the patriotic and the terroristic: "The nation must be taught to be terrified of itself in order to give it courage."[33]

But if Auden were following Marx's recommendation of "ruthless criticism of all that exists" to the letter, he would presumably have been much harder on the schoolboys than he is. What the second ode in fact dramatizes is the enormous emotional difficulty Auden found in criticizing a school life that also stood as his only viable model of political community. In fact, Auden is notably reluctant to apply either weapon or scalpel to the student body he lays out in the second ode. In this pang of conscience, it should be noted, he follows Marx himself: although the characterization of religion as the "heart of the heartless world" is often cited simply as evidence of Marx's anticlericalism, the passage in fact displays a kind of alienated sympathy toward the institution of religion. For Marx, religion expresses the values and interests that would obtain in a utopian social situation, albeit in a mystified form that prevents the people from bringing that situation about. Thus it is "at the same time the expression of real distress and the protest against real distress": a feeling that can (and must) be shared at the same time as the social formations that make it possible must be decisively denounced.

Where Marx indicted the church, Auden substitutes the school: for him, the educational establishment supplies the same kind of false consolation premised on real feeling. Further, by shifting the locus of the "heart of the heartless world" from the church to the school, Auden rejuvenates the trope, since everyone must leave school eventually. As in "Address for a Prize-Day," impending departure from the scholastic environment presents itself, to student and schoolmaster alike, as entry into a "heartless world," a loss of meaningful community and subjection to purely economic forces. Critique of this wider society, formulated from within the relative safety of the academic institution, is ultimately irrelevant to the extramural world outside the school. The schoolboys may be able to take the world's pulse, to diagnose and critique it, but they can't cure or change it: the world is a body unto itself, ridden with its own degenerative diseases, and the school system is not truly its brain, as it likes to imagine, but only, at best, its heart. Similarly, the ways of simple kindness learned in school, the moral habits inculcated by good teachers or sound disciplines, are unlikely to persist long on the outside: "Not as kind as all that; he shall find one fine day he is sold."

In Auden's ode, ecstatic celebration of the school as community confronts a deep-seated skepticism about the school's ability to instill permanent principles and values, on the one hand, or to arm its students with critical weapons against the established norms of society, on the other. The moral decency that the students are able to show as long as they remain within the protected, utopian space of schools like Sedbergh or Larchfield—kindness to servants and fishermen and other members of the lower classes, for instance—will likely dissolve soon after graduation.

Marxist or not, this is a bleak moment in an otherwise giddy poem; the mood of schoolboy glee is in real danger of giving way to the caustic satire found elsewhere in *The Orators* (and in much of Auden's subsequent 1930s work). But the fact that the students' joy is temporary does nothing to undermine the fact of the schoolmaster's authority. Perhaps this is why Auden soon turns away from the larger implications of the Marx passage, focusing instead on the cultivation of the student body by the scrupulous gardener of souls:

From darkness your roses came
In one little week of action
By fortunate prejudice to delighting form
                    And profuse production;
Now about these boys as keen as mustard to grow
Give you leave for that, sir, well in them, flow,
Deep in their wheel-pits may they know you foaming and feel
   you warm.[34]

Here the teacher is likened both to a gardener, tending roses, and to
an engineer installing steam engines (and even, through a playful
use of the Hopkinsian epithet "sir," to God). On one level, then, the
speaker is encouraging the schoolmaster to tend to his students as
gardeners and engineers do to their objects of concern, or to inspire
them as a poet would his readers. "Well in them, flow," the speaker
orders, suggesting at once the shaping work of humanist pedagogy
(the work of "well[ing] in" one's students a sense of virtue, that
which it is good, or "well," to do) and the tropes of divine afflatus
common in Romantic poetry. Even more interestingly, this whole
tropological system is, in principle, reversible: it could, with a few
slight modifications, be made to apply to the students' influence on
their teacher as well as vice versa. That is, the speaker could also be
describing the inspiration that the student body gives to the
schoolmaster-poet (Carritt or Auden). On this reading, the "fortune" belongs to the schoolmaster-poet (who is perhaps also "preju-
diced" toward his favorite students) who is spurred to the "delighting
form" of *poeisis* (a playful parody of Hopkins, for example) and "pro-
fuse production" (a whole suite of odes). The obvious attractions of
the student body—its immediate warmth and presence, its eager-
ness to develop ("keen as mustard to grow"), its passionate desire for
mentors and role models—both inspire the poet to write and give
him ideas about how to market that writing; he has, in both senses,
designs on the student body.

   If these designs in turn produce a sort of shame, it is linked to
Auden's mixed feelings throughout the 1930s about the poet's role
in the establishment of a wider, more inclusive political community.
The revelation of the second ode is that the student body can

constitute such a community, if only temporarily. But the student body is also, for the poet-critic, an audience: the most immediate and perhaps even the only one. It takes nothing away from Auden's genuine concern for the education of English youth to note that in the "Six Odes," and the second in particular, he displays a kind of calculating attitude toward the student culture that had produced him and that seemed likely to provide the most receptive audience for his work.

In *The Orators*, Auden both celebrates the school and recognized it as a sort of cul-de-sac: a closed institution that at once supports the poet-critic—by providing him with a salary, a pool of adoring young admirers, and a perch from which to criticize the culture at large—and fatally limits him. In this, it stands for a whole host of elite institutions that had supported and protected modernism throughout the 1920s. Such institutions, Auden argues, are easily mobilized against outsiders, as his equivalence between school and fascist state suggests. And indeed, in the ensuing decades the state would draw upon the resources of modernism to attack its enemies, as we will see in the next chapter.

4

Interrupting the Muse

BY THE END OF THE 1920S, modernist poet-critics had accrued significant cultural capital. Their books and articles were read by undergraduates and, increasingly, by ambitious graduate students and professors; they participated in seemingly endless symposia on questions of the moment set by little-magazine editors (many of whom were poet-critics themselves); they even occasionally made the newspapers or the slick magazines. Economic capital was another matter, however. The crash of 1929 hit poet-critics as hard as any other group of writers or intellectuals, and in some ways harder. Although the market for fiction did not appreciably contract during the Great Depression, poetry, which was already seen by much of the public (and, perhaps more important, by many publishers and editors) as a luxury good, was threatened by the parlous economic climate. Moreover, the wealthy patrons who had sustained modernist poetry during its first decade of efflorescence began to disappear. Some of them were ruined by the crash, many more were seriously weakened, and some, like the Irish American lawyer John Quinn, who had supported Pound, Yeats, Joyce, and Eliot over the years, simply died, leaving no one in the next generation to replace them.

Fortunately for the beleaguered poet-critics, the Depression—and the attendant expansion of the American welfare state—also created new opportunities for village explainers. The 1930s marked a moment when modernist poet-critics went from being slightly less obscurantist bohemians, charged with clarifying byzantine avant-garde practices to bewildered but sympathetic elites, to being civil servants, charged with reinforcing the ideals and institutions of American democracy and enlisting the energies of art in its defense. Archibald MacLeish—in his time a famous man and a respected poet, now virtually unread—exemplifies this shift. MacLeish was perhaps the most acceptable face modernism could offer to the U.S. establishment in the 1920s and 1930s.[1] Deeply influenced as a poet by Pound, Eliot, and Auden, he was unswervingly modernist in his poetics and his literary tastes. But unlike Eliot the royalist, Pound the fascist, or Auden the fellow traveler, all of whom either fled the United States or lacked original loyalty to it, MacLeish was a solidly patriotic American liberal, and of good WASP stock to boot. Born and raised in the Midwest, educated at Yale and at Harvard Law School, and employed in the early 1930s by *Fortune* and the *New Republic*, MacLeish mixed easily with the kind of elite liberal technocrats who made up Roosevelt's brain trust, and with whom he staffed his administration and New Deal programs.

It's no surprise, then, that MacLeish eventually came to the notice of the president. In 1939 MacLeish, who had no degree in library science or previous government experience, was Roosevelt's unlikely choice to replace the incumbent, Herbert Putnam, as librarian of Congress. Judge Felix Frankfurter's letter of recommendation for MacLeish gives some idea of what the New Dealers perceived as his merits as a candidate: "[MacLeish] unites in himself qualities seldom found in combination—those of the hardheaded lawyer with the sympathetic imagination of the poet, the independent thinker, and the charming 'mixer.' He would bring to the Librarianship intellectual distinction, cultural recognition the world over, a persuasive personality and a delicacy of touch in dealing with others, and creative energy in making the Library of Congress the great center of the cultural resource of the Nation in the technological setting of our time."[2] Frankfurter's letter limns precisely the collection of traits that poet-critics like MacLeish were thought by some forward-thinking members of the American establishment to possess. His virtues were at once artistic (he had "imagination" and was "creative"), interpersonal (he was "sympa-thetic" and "charming" and had "a delicacy of touch in dealing with others"), and pragmatic (he was "hardheaded," "independent," and "persuasive"). They don't teach you these things in library school, and it is clear that when the Roosevelt administration appointed MacLeish, it was looking for something more than a competent upper-level bureaucrat. Appointing MacLeish librarian of Congress was less about stewardship of the nation's libraries than it was about legitimizing state cultural power, bringing the "intellectual distinc-tion" of modernism to what was an institution of otherwise merely "technological" superiority. And MacLeish's ideology, as we will soon see, was almost perfectly in line with the ideas of Roosevelt, Frankfurter, and the other liberal intellectuals who spearheaded the New Deal.

MacLeish, however, needed a little convincing. Replying to Frank-furter in May 1939, he agreed that he "unite[d] in himself qualities seldom found in combination," although he characterized this as a liability rather than a strength: "From the beginning of my more or less adult life I have been plagued by the fact that I seem to be able to do more or less well things which don't commonly go together."[3] But MacLeish, though honored, was anxious about the prospect of accepting a governmental position. "It may be that I have now come to the place in my life where I should stop writing poetry and turn to the public service," he wrote to Frankfurter. "But if I thought so, I am afraid I should not be of much use to the public service, because the one thing I have ever wanted to do with all my heart was to write poetry and the one thing I have ever wanted to be was a poet."[4] MacLeish's letter is Eliotic in its concern that the assumption of a new social duty ("the public service") would leave him no time or energy for the pursuit of poetry. His noblesse oblige was in direct conflict with his modernist faith in the sanctity and importance of art; like the speaker of Eliot's "Gerontion," he feared that he would lose his passion.

Nevertheless, MacLeish eventually agreed to accept the librari-anship on the condition that he be given time to complete his long poem *America Was Promises*, which was already under way. The president wrote MacLeish personally to "guarantee that I will not

interrupt the Muse when she is flirting with you."[5] Here Roosevelt's
rhetoric dovetails perfectly with MacLeish's: the notion of a president
interrupting the Muse in order to enlist a poet's help in the war effort is a high compliment to poetry even as it insists that, in a time
of national crisis, there are more important things. It assumes that a
poet-critic, as a poet-critic, has something vital to contribute to the
protection of democracy. This is exactly what MacLeish had been
insisting over the course of the previous decade.

Granted, he had arrived at this civic-minded position gradually.
In his early years MacLeish was best known as a crusader for the
autonomy of art against the political mobilization of literature by
Marxists and other "revolutionists." In 1932, seven years before his
appointment to the Library of Congress, MacLeish published a
poem in the *New Republic*, "Invocation to the Social Muse," which
took this intransigence as its theme. "Señora, it is true that the
Greeks are dead," the poem begins:

> It is true also that we here are Americans:
> That we use the machines: that a sight of the god is unusual:
> That more people have more thoughts: that there are
>
> Progress and science and tractors and revolutions and
> Marx and the wars more antiseptic and murderous
> And music in every home: there is also Hoover.

MacLeish's speaker, a canny orator, opens with a series of concessions to the would-be revolutionaries: the age of antiquity is past;
we are living in the modern (industrial capitalist) era; we are mostly
secular ("a sight of the god is unusual"); and much of what we see
around us bears out Marx's predictions (including the endurance of
Marxist theory itself). The enumerative style, listing the prosaic
contents of the modern-day United States, is somewhat reminis-
cent of the early Auden, whose ambiguously Communist work
was just beginning to influence American poetry at this time. But
the real message of the poem, it soon becomes clear, is far from the
calls to political action that were the young Auden's specialty. "Does
the lady suggest we should write it out in The Word?" the poem's

speaker asks his Muse. "Does Madame recall our responsibilities?"
But the poet will have none of it:

> We are
> Whores, Fräulein: poets, Fräulein, are persons of
>
> Known vocation following troops: they must sleep with
> Stragglers from either prince and of both views.
> The rules permit them to further the business of neither.

Poets, MacLeish's speaker insists, don't take sides; or rather, they
take every side: they attach themselves temporarily to one prince or
another, whoring with the powerful but giving nothing of themselves and ultimately furthering the business of no one. Such
political promiscuity is a survival tactic, but real poetry, he goes
on to say, transcends fashionable causes and gravitates always
toward transhistorical universals:

> There are only a handful of things a man likes,
> Generation to generation, hungry or
>
> Well fed: the earth's one: life's
> One: Mister Morgan is not one.
> There is nothing worse for our trade than to be in style.

After pausing to take a parenthetical swipe at Pound and his followers ("(Who recalls the address now of the Imagists?)"), Mac-
Leish's speaker insists that poets are meant to focus only on human
frailty and individual experience:

> The naked man has always his own nakedness.
> People remember forever his live limbs.
> The things of the poet are done to a man alone
> As the things of love are done—or of death when he hears the
> Step withdraw on the stair and the clock tick only.

Love and death are proper subjects for poetry, but not war or
revolution. In the poem's final lines, the military implications of the

term "avant-garde"—which, by 1932, would evoke the Trotskyist Left as much as any tradition of experimental art and writing—are summarily refused: "I remind you, the life of the poet is hard. . . . / Is it just to demand of us also to bear arms?"[6]

"Invocation to the Social Muse" established MacLeish's early 1930s position as an anti-ideological aesthete, but by the end of the decade he had moved from resisting the pressure on poets to declare overt political allegiances to shaming those who remained uncommitted to the cause of antifascism. (See, for instance, "The Affirmation," his contribution to a May 1939 issue of *Survey Graphic:* "I believe that American liberalism must accept the full obligation of its decision to defend democracy against fascism.")[7] The key text marking this evolution is "The Irresponsibles," first issued as a pamphlet in 1940 and reprinted the following year in *A Time to Speak*, a mass-market collection of his essays. In it, MacLeish attacks writers and scholars for failing to adequately respond to the rise of totalitarian nation-states and their "destruction of writing and of scholarship."[8] The martial tropes of "Invocation to the Social Muse" return as MacLeish recalls that "certain young novelists and poets, the most generous and gallant of their time, gave up their lives as writers and enlisted in the hopeless armies to fight brutality with force."[9] The sacrifice that MacLeish, in "Invocation to the Social Muse," had deemed improper is here wholeheartedly recommended. Note that MacLeish does not say simply that these novelists and poets "gave up their lives"; he says that they "gave up their lives as writers." The uncommitted life of the pure, autonomous artist—the life described in "Invocation to the Social Muse"—was exactly what, in MacLeish's terms, needed to be sacrificed for the sake of civilization, just as he had (temporarily) sacrificed his poetic career to devote himself to "the public service": not because political catastrophe had proven aesthetic autonomy to be illusory (as Marxist critics claimed), but precisely because such autonomy was real and precious.

Against the writers who selfishly or obliviously continue to live their lives as writers, MacLeish posits a heroic, civic-minded man of letters: "The man of intellectual *office*, the man of intellectual *calling*, the man who *professes* letters—professes an obligation as a servant of the mind to defend the mind's integrity against every physical power—professes an obligation to defend the labors of the mind and the structures it has created and the means by which it lives, not only privately and safely in his study, not only strictly and securely in the controversies of the learned press, but publicly and at the public risk and danger of his life."[10] It is typical of MacLeish's language of the time that his heroic man of letters is both highly distinguished (a "man of intellectual *office*") and humble ("a servant of the mind"). To work for democracy and oppose fascism, Mac-Leish suggests, is both a renunciation and a promotion: an opportunity for poets to put aside being unacknowledged legislators of the world for a while and do some acknowledged legislation for a change.

In "The Irresponsibles," MacLeish conspicuously reverses several of his earlier positions. Whereas "Invocation to the Social Muse" had insisted that poets were whores, not soldiers, here Mac-Leish asserts that poets—in fact, poetry—are one of the enemies on whom fascists (and, to a lesser extent, Communists) have declared war. Fascism is presented as a threat to liberal individualism and to the Enlightenment: "This crisis is in essence a cultural crisis—a revolt of certain classes, certain conditions of men against the inherited culture of the West and against all common culture—a revolt by no means limited to those nations alone where it has been successful," he warns. He emphasizes the anti-intellectual aspects of the Third Reich: "Without this attack upon the habits of the mind, the reliances of the spirit, that revolution could not, by any possibility, have succeeded." Poets have never been at war before, but now they must be, because they and their culture have been directly attacked: "How could we sit back as spectators of a war against ourselves?"[11]

"The Irresponsibles" falls squarely into the genre that Mark Greif (writing of similar discourses dating from the same era, which he terms "the Age of the Crisis of Man") has called "maieutic discourse": a style of discourse that, "by insistent and forceful questioning, seeks to bring into being and bring to birth *in another person* answers that will reward the questioner's own belief in the character of the universal capacity for thinking—and do something to the other person's character, too."[12] Maieutic discourse sets the terms of others' discussions, gives people something to talk about, and suggests that they are failing, morally, should they decline to address it. "The perversion of the mind is only possible when those who should be heard in its defense are silent," MacLeish writes, and his intention here is precisely to prevent them from being silent. This is necessary, he explains, because the modernist obsession with aesthetic autonomy (like the scholar's pursuit of academic freedom) have separated intellectuals from what matters most to their ultimate survival. "The artist does not fight," MacLeish reflects ruefully. "The artist's obligations are to his art. His responsibility—his one responsibility—is to his art. He has no other." All well and good: this is what modernist autonomy is supposed to be all about, after all. But there are consequences, dire ones, to the fact that "both writers and scholars freed themselves of the personal responsibility associated with personal choice. They emerged free, pure and single into the antiseptic air of objectivity. And by that sublimation of the mind they prepared the mind's disaster."[13]

The distance traveled from "Invocation to the Social Muse" to "The Irresponsibles" is considerable, but it is also easily explained as a reaction to the course of historical events from 1932 to 1939. Hitler was sworn in as chancellor in January 1933; the next month, arsonists set fire to the Reichstag building in Berlin, an act that led to the suspension of civil liberties in Germany and the construction of the first concentration camps. The Nazi Party (and, in Italy, Mussolini's Fascists) consolidated power over the course of the 1930s and began to expand their empires; in 1938 German soldiers slaughtered almost one hundred Jews. It would have been strange if MacLeish had not reconsidered his ideas about the relationship between poetry and politics during this period, and indeed, many of his contemporaries went through a similar (though less public) process of conversion to a more politicized position.

But MacLeish's rhetoric of sacrifice in texts like "The Irresponsibles" was also connected to a social democratic (that is, nonrevolutionary) critique of capitalism. Ira Katznelson and other historians of the New Deal have shown how the liberals who populated Roosevelt's cabinet and supported his policies were nearly as terrified of

Marxism and totalitarianism on the left as they were of fascism.[14] They saw the threat to democracy as emanating from Nazi Germany and Fascist Italy but also from the Soviet Union and even from the radical labor movement rapidly gaining ground at home. MacLeish shared these broad fears and also the New Dealers' assumption that the solution must come from above. In the 1930s and 1940s he was animated, as Michael Augspurger noted, by "a fundamental belief in the leadership role of the professional managerial class."[15] The corollary to this belief was a critique of selfish apolitical elites who had shirked this leadership role, a critique that could, depending on the context, be directed at either economic or cultural elites. Throughout the 1930s MacLeish criticized the capitalist class and modernist writers in very similar terms: as elites who had abdicated their responsibility to the public. In a 1935 essay titled "A Stage for Poetry," for instance, MacLeish lamented poetry's lack of ambition and scope, which he linked explicitly to its dwindling aristocratic means of support:

> Poetry cannot continue in its present state; if it attempts to do so it will die and the obsequies will pass unnoticed. An art which lives by the production of little books to lie on little tables; an art which must be cherished by foundations and female societies and literary prizes; an art which is appreciated only by the peculiarly sensitive or the delicately lonely or the deeply passionate, is not an art in flower. To flourish, an art must touch the general mind of its time—not merely the most sensitive minds of its time. Poetry has lost that touch.[16]

This rhetoric was not altogether new; many of the alarmist notes MacLeish sounded about the imminent death or disappearance of poetry dated back, as John Timberman Newcomb has demonstrated, to the 1890s.[17] Other details are more specifically modernist: the disparagement of "sensitive minds" hearkens back to Eliot's essays of the late 1910s and early 1920s, and the reference to "female societies" adapts a well-worn Poundian attack on the feminization of poetry. Most striking, though, is the reference to "little books to lie on little tables," which obviously targets the small presses and little magazines that had been the primary venues for modernist poetry up to this point (and to which MacLeish had often contributed). Modernist poetry, MacLeish alleges, has settled for too little and allowed itself to become detached from "the general mind of its time" by accepting handouts from "foundations and female societies." A manlier and more moral brand of modernism would eschew such support and find a way to reconnect with Americans of all classes and educational levels.

In place of the ineffectual "little" ventures with which his contemporaries were content, MacLeish dreamed of a version of modernism blown up to national—and international—scale, allied with the nearly unbounded executive power of the American presidency in the New Deal era. He had already voiced his admiration for Roosevelt (who had not yet assumed office) a year earlier in a piece for the *Forum* titled "Preface to an American Manifesto." "Let no man miss the point of Mr. Roosevelt's hold upon the minds of the citizens of this republic," MacLeish writes. "Men's minds are fired by Mr. Roosevelt because they are sick to nausea of the rich bankers and their economists upon the one side and the wise revolutionaries and their economists upon the other, repeating over and over that the world is ruled by incontrovertible economic laws which it is not only blasphemy but idiocy to oppose, and which lead inevitably to certain fixed and inescapable conclusions."[18]

For liberal progressives like MacLeish, Roosevelt's presidency represented a way to curb the excesses of capitalism and harness populist antibusiness sentiment without advocating Communist revolution and thus, potentially, setting the stage for a totalitarian U.S. government similar to that which had emerged in the Soviet Union. But in this battle for the hearts and minds of the American people, MacLeish realized, his beloved modernism had taken the wrong side: the side of an irresponsible capitalism. In *America Was Promises*, the long poem he was struggling to finish when Roosevelt called him up to serve as librarian of Congress, MacLeish reflected on the decadence of the American cultural elite:

> The Aristocracy of Wealth and Talents
> Turned its talents into wealth and lost them.
> Turned enlightened selfishness to wealth.

Turned self-interest into bankbooks: balanced them.
Bred out: bred to fools: to hostlers:
Card sharps: well dressed women: dancefloor doublers.
The Aristocracy of Wealth and Talents
Sold its talents: bought the public notice:
Drank in public: went to bed in public:
Patronized the arts in public: pall'd with
Public authors public beauties; posed in
Public postures for the public page.

The Aristocracy of Wealth and Talents
Moved out: settled on the Continent:
Sat beside the water at Rapallo:
Died in a rented house: unwept: unhonored.

What is interesting here is the virtual identity MacLeish assumes between artists and their patrons: he juxtaposes the self-interested capitalists who "turned enlightened selfishness to wealth" to modernist émigrés who have "settled on the Continent." (The reference to Rapallo makes it obvious that he is thinking of Pound, although the "rented house" may also be a subtle allusion to Eliot's "Gerontion.") Both kinds of aristocracies, MacLeish implies—that of "Wealth" and that of "Talents"—have acted irresponsibly by prioritizing their own interests above the general welfare of the nation-state; in this way, if not in others, they are one and the same. The poem ends with a passionate exhortation:

> Listen! Brothers! Generation!
> . . .
> Listen! Believe the speaking dead! Believe
> The journey is our journey. Oh believe
> The signals were to us: the signs: the birds by
> Night: the breaking surf.
>
> Believe
>
> America is promises to
> Take!
> America is promises to

Us
To take them
Brutally
With love but
Take them.
Oh believe this![19]

Along with the expected American exceptionalism and sense of divine predestination ("the signals were to us"), there is weirdly violent, sexual imagery, suggestive of a marital rape: "Take them/Brutally/With love but/Take them." Poets are no longer the passive "whores" who flit from prince to prince; now they are the aggressors, the powerful men who must seize America and its promises for its own good.

America Was Promises was published in 1939 to mixed reviews. Meanwhile, MacLeish had assumed his duties as librarian of Congress, and he would go on to serve the Roosevelt administration in various capacities, as director of the War Department's Office of Facts and Figures and assistant director of the Office of War Information. The year 1939, then, is as good a year as any to date the emergence of what Greg Barnhisel calls "Cold War modernism," a formation that would reach its apogee in the 1950s, when "modernism [was] used in support of Western middle-class society" and became an instrument of cultural diplomacy for the U.S. government. Barnhisel identifies MacLeish, alongside Nelson Rockefeller, as one of the major figures in this movement to recast modernism as a bulwark of liberalism, individualism, and even capitalism (all values it had explicitly attacked in its earlier iterations). "Even as it retained its associations with innovation and the drive for the new, modernism also came to be presented as a pro-Western, pro-'freedom,' and pro-bourgeois movement, evidence of the superiority of the Western way of life," Barnhisel writes. "Largely emptied of content, modernism as a style retained its prestige and status, particularly among intellectuals."[20]

MacLeish's official involvement with the Roosevelt administration, coupled with his passionate and reasoned arguments for writers and scholars to become more engaged in the fight against fascism, marked the beginning of this turn toward a bigger, emptier modernism. In a way, he used the status of the modernist poet-critic to evacuate the ideology that poet-critics had constructed, an ideology that prized aesthetic autonomy over political engagement, was suspicious of liberalism and the cult of the individual, and regarded capitalism and the market with cold contempt. If MacLeish and other Cold War modernists were not quite successful in filling the empty vessel of modernism with the opposite of these values—a public-spirited patriotism, a respect for personal freedom, and a belief in the civilizing influence of free enterprise—he nonetheless made it possible for powerful people who did hold liberal beliefs to claim modernism as a public good and to overlook its more illiberal or apolitical aspects.

❧ ❧ ❧

Poet-critics worked for the federal government for many reasons during the 1930s. Some were doubtless moved by the eloquence of patriots like MacLeish, but the most immediate and probably most common reason was economic relief. Modernist writers, like other Americans, were financially hobbled and chronically unemployed, and those who had not committed to a posture of radical opposition to the Roosevelt administration were happy to accept the wages that government jobs provided. The most beneficial program for poet-critics and other insolvent modernists was the Federal Writers' Project (FWP), instituted in September 1935 as part of the Works Progress Administration (WPA). Although the FWP was not specifically geared toward poets (or even toward established authors), it nevertheless employed a host of poet-critics, including Conrad Aiken, R. P. Blackmur, Malcolm Cowley, Weldon Kees, Claude McKay, and Kenneth Rexroth.

In addition to the invaluable financial assistance it provided to unemployed writers during some of the worst years of the Depression, then, the FWP is remarkable for the way it collapsed social distinctions—always tenuous—between different types and classes of writers. "[Henry] Alsberg [director of the FWP] wrestled with the question of how to define *writer*," the historian Michael Hiltzik notes, "a term that could embrace doggerel poets, advertising copywriters, and newspaper scribes, as well as novelists of transcendent craftsmanship. Since the number of available nonfiction and technical writers vastly outstripped writers of real refinement, he decided to unify his motley staff by focusing them on a single overarching project. The result would be the WPA Guides, a monumental collection of 152 state, local, and city guidebooks."[21] Michael Szalay makes a similar point in *New Deal Modernism:* "Because it was not clear before the advent of the WPA what made a writer a 'professional,' it was doubly unclear how to consider the employment status of writers who had never been successful to begin with."[22]

The FWP, and the Guide series in particular, provided a kind of lowest common denominator for unemployed writers and intellectuals of all kinds: poets, novelists, journalists, critics, and social scientists could all be put to use. These were populist initiatives that, by their very design, were incompatible with the charismatic hierarchies that usually structure literary culture. Such programs "would employ not only established artists and talented novices, but also the worker ants of the cultural world—technicians, journeymen, craftspersons," Michael Hiltzik writes. "There had been government arts programs before . . . but these typically involved established artists whose works were selected by professional juries. The historian and critic Bernard DeVoto, looking back on the Federal Writers' Project in 1942, observed 'without any shadow of derogation' that 'most of the people employed by the Project have never been, even in the humblest sense, genuine writers. . . . It has been, in fact, a project for research workers.' "[23]

But the FWP offered more to writers—and to modernist poet-critics in particular—than temporary employment. Political populists who were not sufficiently radical to eschew collaboration with the state in a capitalist society (left-liberals, in other words, who were not decisively aligned with either anarchism or Marxism) could slip mildly subversive content past the government censors. Mandarin modernists who cared for aesthetic autonomy above all could, for a brief window, get the nation-state to fund work that had previously relied on the support of patrons. Finally, women, writers of color, and other people ordinarily marginalized within literary culture had an unprecedented—if limited and coincidental—opportunity to participate in American literary and cultural life.[24]

The situation was especially complex for African American writers. Black writers had been a vital force within modernism throughout the 1920s; the productions of the Harlem Renaissance were both influenced by white modernists and influenced them in turn, and African American influence (however facetiously or offensively absorbed) was a virtual sine qua non for avant-garde literature in the high modernist period, particularly in the United States. In the 1930s, however, the culture of literary modernism began to fracture along racial lines as black writers (who, like all Americans of color, suffered far more from the effects of the Depression than whites) became increasingly radicalized.

It was thus absolutely crucial for the federal government to enlist African American intellectual leaders in order to legitimize itself among the black population and allay suspicions that state relief was to be provided only to whites. Black intellectuals already had a very different relation to the federal government than their white counterparts, in some ways more suspicious and adversarial, in other ways closer. Government jobs were some of the most prestigious and lucrative positions available to African Americans in the early twentieth century; racial discrimination, while still pronounced, was considerably less so in government (at the federal rather than the state level) than in many industries. For black writers and intellectuals in the Jim Crow era, government work could be seen not as service or sacrifice to a greater national good but as a form of enfranchisement. But the agenda and priorities of the American government at both the state and federal levels were often at odds with those of the African American intelligentsia, and those who worked in government were always vulnerable to accusations of compromise and betrayal from the black community at large. It is crucial to bear this context in mind when one considers the long, strange bureaucratic journey of the poet-critic Sterling A. Brown.

On June 19, 1928, the sociologist Charles S. Johnson wrote to Brown praising his recent poetry. At a time when many of his contemporaries were settling in Harlem and enjoying the benefits of a lively, close-knit intellectual society, Brown was building his academic career by traveling around the American South, teaching at various agrarian institutions. The result was that Brown, though roughly the same age as prominent Harlem Renaissance writers like Langston Hughes and Wallace Thurman, was getting a slightly later start in the acquisition of literary fame. But in the process, Johnson suggested, he had obtained other advantages. "You have been compensated for your period of teaching in Virginia and Missouri by a command of the Negro folk idiom which is truly delightful," Johnson wrote:

> I was remarking to [Countee] Cullen the other day that I felt that your poetry has shown the most distinctive and superior contribution of any of the younger writers since 1926. It seems to me that there is a great struggle, even among the most brilliant ones of that earlier period, 1922–1926, against going to seed. I wondered if it is to be the fate of many of them to flash early and die. One hope lies in getting in contact with the actual source material and in keeping abreast of the best that is being done in the world of letters. You have a distinct advantage here and, unquestionably, you are using it.[25]

Despite Johnson's reassurance that Brown's fieldwork, as it were, was having a salutary effect on his poetry, there is no question that Brown's distance from Harlem and other urban centers of African American culture, as well as his academic affiliations, made a decisive difference in the course of his career. As Lawrence Jackson puts it in *The Indignant Generation*, "Brown's early success as a poet seemed nearly secondary to his career as a professional advocate of black arts."[26] In addition to sheaves of critical articles and reviews for little magazines like *Opportunity* and the *Crisis*, Brown composed teacher's guides (his 1931 "Outline for the Study of Poetry of American Negroes" was one of the first on this subject), worked from 1938 to 1940 on the landmark Gunnar Myrdal study of race relations in America, and, in the 1940s, coedited mass-market anthologies like *The Negro Caravan* and *A Primer for White Folks*. Although he was often identified and acclaimed as a poet—and a highly influential, and important one—Brown published just one book of poetry in the first seventy years of his life: 1927's *Southern Road*. While many of his peers, Johnson and Cullen among them, expected him to be one of the great poets of his generation, Brown's contribution to the collective project of African American literature would prove to be primarily critical and administrative rather than creative or literary.

Not that the two were cleanly or easily separable. Johnson's description of Brown's work as "getting in contact with the source material" points to a specifically anthropological aspect of the latter's poetics. Brown, though born and raised in Washington, D.C., to middle-class parents, styled himself as a folk poet. Whereas most Harlem-based writers dwelt on urban and cosmopolitan subjects, Brown was committed to documenting the diction and customs of African Americans living in rural areas. The question of the relation between the rising, urbanized African American middle class and the predominantly rural, working-class "folk" population was a crucial one for Brown. In essays for *Opportunity* like "Our Literary Audience" (1930), he rails against unflattering depictions of the folk in African American literature and asserted that "the dominance of the lowly as subject matter is a natural concomitant to the progress of democracy." In the same essay, he takes issue with the black intelligentsia's "distaste for dialect," which had fallen out of favor with "respectable" Negro audiences shortly after the heyday of Paul Laurence Dunbar: "There is nothing 'degraded' about dialect. Dialectical peculiarities are universal. There is something about Negro dialect, in the idiom, the turn of the phrase, the music of the vowels and consonants that is worth treasuring." Brown's full-throated defense of dialect formed part of a larger challenge to the black bourgeois readers of journals like *Opportunity* to overcome their sense of cultural shame and reconnect with their folk heritage:

> It seems to acute observers that many of us, who have leisure for reading, are ashamed of being Negroes. This shame makes us harsher to the shortcomings of some perhaps not so fortunate economically. There seems to be among us a more fundamental lack of sympathy with the Negro farthest down, than there is in other groups with the same Negro. . . . We are cowed.

We have become typically bourgeois. Natural though such an
evolution is, if we are *all* content with evasion of life, with personal complacency, we as a group are doomed. If we pass by on
the other side, despising our brothers, we have no right to call
ourselves men.[27]

Brown's appeal to the folk against the middle class was, in certain
respects, conventional for his time. In his 1926 essay "The Negro
Artist and the Racial Mountain," for instance, Langston Hughes
scorns the member of "the Negro middle class" who "is never taught
to see . . . the beauty of his own people [but is] taught not to see it,
or if he does, to be ashamed of it." In response to this bourgeois
blindness, Hughes exalts "the low-down folks, the so-called common
element."[28] But Brown's academically mediated interest in folk
culture was qualitatively different from the romanticization of
working-class life in which Harlem Renaissance writers sometimes
indulged. Brown, while attracted to Hughes's poetic populism, re-
sisted the demagogic terms of an essay like "The Negro Artist and
the Racial Mountain." He, too, was deeply interested in the life of
rural lower-class African Americans of whom "the Negro middle
class" tended to be ashamed. But whereas Hughes wanted to claim
African American modernist poetry—or, at least, his own work—as
something directly and authentically of the people, better understood by "the low-down folks" than by bourgeois sophisticates,
Brown tended to emphasize a kind of institutional distance between
the black middle-class poet-critic and the "low-down folks" he ob-
serves and describes.

It may be easiest to see how this works by attending to a poem
since, as is often the case with poet-critics, the anxieties that Brown
resolved into dogmas or precepts in his literary and cultural criticism are manifested and dramatized in poems. Many of the poems
in *Southern Road* adopt what I call an "ethnographic lyric" mode
that combines the sociological or anthropological techniques of interview and observation with the kind of African American vernacular forms being developed by writers like Hughes and welds them
together via the traditional English form of the dramatic monologue. The best example of Brown's ethnographic lyric mode is his

first published poem, 'When de Saints Go Ma'ching Home," which narrates an encounter between Brown and its subject and dedicatee, the itinerant worker and sometime vagrant Big Boy Davis, whom he met through his students at Virginia Seminary College in the mid-1920s. "The kids at Seminary knew my interest," Brown recounts in a 1974 interview with Charles H. Rowell:

> I was writing these poems, and they brought [him] to my room one night. . . . My room was a gathering place for bull sessions, because these students were about my age. They were old to be in school, and I was young to be out of school. They were coal miners, farmers, hard workers, waiters down at the hotel. This was called Virginia Seminary College. Many of them were studying to be ministers, but they had to work like hell in order to make enough money to come for those school months. So these kids knew my interest, and they brought Big Boy to the room. . . . He was an education for me.[29]

We should pause to consider the rather elaborate social, economic, and academic dynamics in play here. On one side, we have Sterling Brown, the upper-middle-class professor, product of the elite Dunbar High School in Washington, D.C., Williams College, and Harvard University. On the other, we have the student seminarians (the same age as Brown or older) from rather humbler backgrounds, aspiring to enter the middle class by studying to be ministers. They provide Brown with a conduit to Big Boy, a poor laborer with no apparent interest in upward mobility, to whom someone of Brown's class background might not have otherwise had easy access. (The poem's epigraph tells us that Davis was later "chased out of town for vagrancy.") The "education" that Brown claims Big Boy gave him, and that one would normally assume would be passed down from teacher to student to nonstudent, in fact circulates much more complexly here. Big Boy's very name encodes confusion about whether he was a student or a teacher. The speaker of the poem is presumably Brown himself, but it could just as easily be one of his seminary students: no distinction is made in the poem between him and them; the group is always referred to in the plural, as "we" or "the boys." Everyone assembled here is a "boy," but everyone is also a potential master: everyone is capable of teaching everyone else something, and in fact it is the least educationally credentialed person present (Big Boy) who possesses the most valuable knowledge in this situation (the blues).

Unlike some of the other poems in *Southern Road*, "When de Saints Go Ma'ching Home" is not a straightforward blues poem. Indeed, it seems to provide an especially striking example of what Brent Hayes Edwards sees as "the specific effect of the blues poem," which he argued is "rooted precisely in its *not* being the 'same' as the vernacular blues. . . . It is a reduction of the poem to relegate it to the status of a song lyric. It demands to be considered as much a formal *transcription* of a performance . . . as a *score* to be realized."[30] "When de Saints Go Ma'ching Home" makes this act of lyric transcription described by Edwards part of the structure of the work itself: it is a description of a transcription, putting us at a double remove from the song itself. The poem begins in medias res, toward the end of a longer series of musical performances by Big Boy:

> He'd play, after the bawdy songs and blues,
> After the weary plaints
> Of "Trouble, Trouble deep down in muh soul,"
> Always one song in which he'd lose the role
> Of entertainer to the boys. He'd say
> "My mother's favorite." And we knew
> That what was coming was his chant of saints
> "When de Saints go ma'chin' home . . ."
> And that would end his concert for the day.

What does it mean here that Big Boy is "los[ing] the role / Of entertainer to the boys"? "Losing" it by failing to entertain them or (more likely) forgetting that entertainment is his goal and drifting into a genuine reverie? Further, when he loses the role of entertainer, what does he become? A teacher? A case study? A cautionary tale?

That some kind of transformation of Big Boy's role, and of his relationship to his auditors, is taking place is further suggested by the start of the second stanza:

Carefully as an old maid over needlework,
Or, as some black deacon, over his Bible, lovingly,
He'd tune up specially for this. There'd be
No chatter now, no patting of the feet
After a few slow chords, knelling and sweet . . .
He would forget
The quieted bunch, his dimming cigarette
Stuck into a splintered edge of the guitar;
Sorrow deep hidden in his voice, a far
And soft light in his strange brown eyes,
Alone with his masterchords, his memories.

Behind the surface sentimentalism of Brown's tone, we can trace Big Boy's surprising metamorphoses: first, he's feminized ("an old maid over needlework"), and then he takes on a religious authority ("some black deacon"). His performance is clearly designated as such ("He'd tune up specially") but also seems to transcend the context of mere performance as he "forgets" his audience and stands "alone with his masterchords, his memories."

All throughout these early stanzas we are preparing to listen to Big Boy's song: Brown is slowly ceding the floor to him in anticipation of letting him fill the space of the poem with his own expression. But, at the same time, we are observing him from an ethnographic remove: Big Boy is figured as a mystery, with "sorrow deep hidden in his voice," his "strange brown eyes." (The echo of Brown's family name appears continually throughout the poems in *Southern Road;* and Big Boy is precisely a strange Brown, an uncanny double of the poet himself.) Thereafter, the poem shifts into and out of dialect, using both free indirect discourse and quotation to render Big Boy's speech patterns and idiom:

The chap's few speeches helped me understand
The reason why he gazed so fixedly
Upon the burnished strings.
For he would see
A gorgeous procession to "de Beulah Land"
Of Saints—his friends—*"a climbin, fo' deir wings."*

Oh, when de saints go ma'chin' home
Lawd, I wanna be one o' dat nummer
When de saints goa ma'chin' home.

This takes us from the very Anglo-inflected "chap's few speeches" and "the burnished strings" (with its self-consciously literary echo of *Antony and Cleopatra*, as well as Eliot's *Waste Land*) to the likes of *"a climbin, fo' deir wings,"* cleverly stitching together two different dialects—and social classes—with the thread of a rhyme. Unlike Hughes and other Harlem poets who ventriloquize the speech of the black underclass, Brown never lets us forget the presence of the college boys and the middle-class professor in the room with Big Boy; his voice is never given more than a few full lines to itself.

The poem ends with Big Boy taking his leave of the boys in a brief six-line section:

> He'd shuffle off from us, always; at that,—
> His face a brown study beneath his torn brimmed hat.
> His broad shoulders slouching, his old box strung
> Around his neck;—he'd go where we
> Never could follow him—to Sophie probably,
> Or to his dances in old Tinbridge flat.[31]

The expression "to be in a brown study" (already almost archaic by 1927) dates back to fourteenth-century England and describes a state of melancholy, pensiveness, or reflectiveness. It functions here to jolt us out of Big Boy's idiom—not that we had ever fully settled there—and back into the speaker's: Big Boy himself, presumably, would not use or even know such a high-toned phrase. But note that the speaker doesn't say that Big Boy looks like he's in "a brown study"; he says that Big Boy's face *is* a brown study, as in a case study, a study in brownness. Here again we have the echo of Brown's own name, at once linking him to Big Boy, the authentic voice of the folk, and distinguishing them from each other. The brief moment of communion between "the boys" and Big Boy has given way to an inevitable social separation: "He'd go where we / Never could follow him." (They could, but presumably at the risk of breaking social or ethical taboos; we've already heard that Sophie, Big Boy's lady friend, would be expelled from Heaven, so we can only imagine the effect she'd have on a bunch of seminary students.)

The thwarted desire to follow Big Boy and other members of the folk and the difficulty or impossibility of doing so constitute one of the major themes of *Southern Road.* If Big Boy is a subject of ethnographic study, he is also, here and elsewhere, an exemplary figure to be imitated or followed. Indeed, Brown was deeply admiring throughout the book of the labor that stoic African American men like Big Boy (the "strong men," as he admiringly called them in another poem) performed.[32] But of course Brown could never really be like Big Boy, nor, if it meant sacrificing the economic and social privileges his family had gained over time, did he actually want to. What could be done, then, by the middle-class black intellectual trying to resist bourgeois embarrassment about the lower classes, on the one hand, and unseemly imitation of their idioms and customs, on the other?

The answer is implicit in Brown's treatment of his material in "When de Saints Go Ma'chin' Home" and other ethnographic lyrics in *Southern Road:* one must study the folk and insist on their fitness as a subject to be studied. This helps explain Brown's gravitation toward the social sciences in the 1920s, a field that, thanks in part to the pioneering efforts of W. E. B. Du Bois, was allowing African Americans to be the scholars as well as the subjects—a transition that literary criticism, as Brown consistently pointed out in his early essays, had yet to accomplish. In his early essay "Negro Character as Seen by White Authors" (first printed in the *Journal of Negro Education* in 1933), Brown insists that "if one wishes to learn of *the* Negro, it would be best to study *the* Negro himself. . . . It is likely that . . . the exploration of Negro life and character rather than its exploitation must come from Negro authors themselves."[33] It is only through an interdisciplinary combination of literature and social science that the Du Boisian standard of "the race man" could be carried forward into the future. The social sciences (sociology, anthropology, and the study of folklore) allowed African American scholars to study their own culture while also continuing to serve as exemplars to their communities; black sociologists like Du Bois,

Johnson, and E. Franklin Frazier were simultaneously bourgeois success stories and radical antagonists of bourgeois complacency. By being black scholars studying black culture—particularly working-class black culture—they helped legitimate their own racial and cultural identity as an object worthy of professional academic study.

But of course, professional academic study necessarily occurs within professional academic institutions. Brown's commitment to studying, and not simply celebrating, folk culture had political entailments that insulated him against the radical anti-institutional turn taken by many of the Harlem writers. It is significant that Brown did almost all his work, both artistic and political, from within the framework of large bureaucratic institutions such as the Federal Writers' Project, the Carnegie Foundation (which supported the Myrdal study), and historically black universities like Lincoln, Fisk, and Howard. For Brown, a meaningful connection between the black bourgeoisie and the working classes was made possible only through the intervention of institutions like the university and the state, and the ascendance of a black elite to positions of white-collar respectability. By participating wholeheartedly and unreservedly in institutional life, the black intellectual could ascend the social ladder while continuing to keep a weather eye on folk culture, not forgetting or being ashamed of his folk heritage but, on the contrary, cultivating it as a legitimate field of study.

ⱷⱷⱷ ⱷⱷⱷ ⱷⱷⱷ

The expertise that Brown accumulated in the field as both professor and poet-critic in the 1920s soon led him into other pastures entirely. The 1930s were a boom time for the collection of African American folk materials, during which the federal government subsidized the work of white folklorists like Benjamin Botkin and Alan Lomax under the aegis of the Library of Congress. In 1935 the FWP launched its series of state guides, and director Henry Alsberg, at the suggestion of prominent African American intellectuals like Alain Locke and James Weldon Johnson, tapped Brown as "editor of Negro affairs" for the entire project. In 1937 the FWP began conducting a series of interviews with over two thousand former slaves, contributing to a corpus of texts that would later be titled the Slave Narrative Collection.

Brown, as Locke and Johnson must have realized, was an ideal fit for the FWP in that his literary work was overtly anthropological and research based in a way that was directly applicable to the program's goals. Yet, as a regular contributor to black-edited little magazines like the *Crisis* and *Opportunity*, he also possessed prestige in African American literary and intellectual circles. This prestige was important because it gave the projects in which Brown was involved a veneer of both academic seriousness and political righteousness. To a certain extent, the guides and the Slave Narrative Collection, like most of the activities conducted under Federal One, were make-work, undertaken simply to give employment to the unemployed and stimulate areas of the country that were suffering particularly badly in the Depression economy. But there was also a larger nationalist agenda at stake. In "Sterling Brown and the Dialect of New Deal Optimism," Todd Carmody suggests that the collection of these anthropological materials, especially the interviews with ex-slaves, "appropriate[s] black vernacular speech for a liberal agenda of cultural renewal. The black voice . . . not only sanctions revisionist history [by distorting the narrative of African-American under slavery and in the Jim Crow era], it also becomes part of an optimistic view of nationalist futurity."[34] Brown's affiliation with the FWP, then, would serve a legitimizing function similar to that of MacLeish's appointment at the Library of Congress, transforming what Carmody calls "administrative appropriation, or bureaucratic blackface" into something that would appear to African American intellectuals as an authentically progressive literary and political project.

Brown, for his part, felt considerable hesitation about accepting a position within the FWP. "I have been up to my neck in work during the past year," he replied to Alsberg in 1936, "school work, finishing up a couple of books, which will not finish, and directing dramatics (a full job in itself). . . . I was surprised at my appointment, and not sure of my ability to handle this large undertaking. I want to get as much advice as possible. . . . I want advice upon the material relating to the Negro that should be included in the *American*

Guide, and available, qualified people who might help in the project, either as workers or advisors."[35] With his African American friends Brown was even more candid about his trepidations. "[This is] a cry from Macedonia—'Come on over and help us,'" he wrote to Johnson, who was then on the national advisory board for the WPA, in May 1936. "I am serving as editor of Negro material on the *American Guide* [*sic*]. I have no illusions about my editorial ability."[36] Still, Brown recognized the historic opportunity that the program represented. "The advantages of such a project are numerous," he wrote. "In the first place material that will be more authentic will be on hand to offset some of the stuff probably being written, and a few more Negroes, who can certify, may get jobs."[37]

It appears that Brown's reasons for accepting the FWP job were both ideological and practical. He clearly felt that he had an opportunity to dispel certain deeply entrenched misunderstandings about African American life and culture: in effect, to instrumentalize the criticisms he had been advancing in the pages of the *Crisis* and *Opportunity* about the corrosive effects of negative racial stereotypes. At the same time, the project would allow him to employ friends, students, and colleagues who had been suffering under the Depression, and it would help bring legitimacy and financial support to the underfunded black academic institutions that had sustained his career to date. Writing to Charles Jones of the National Urban League in January 1939 in defense of the Federal Arts Projects, then under attack from a congressional committee formed by Representative Martin Dies to ferret out Communists within Federal One, Brown admits that

> as far as the Negro is concerned, these projects, of course, still leave something to be desired. Employment of Negroes, especially in the South, is far too little. Discrimination in rank and salary has taken place. . . . But in the main the projects have great importance for a number (not large enough) of Negro artists, research workers, etc. The projects afford one of the Negro's important opportunities for work in the white collar field. . . . I know that the Project has given employment to needy Negroes who otherwise would have had little or no chance

to use their training and ability. These people in many cases developed skill, learned a great deal, and made definite contributions to the charting of America.[38]

Here we see a dual justification for Brown's support—and, by implication, the support of the black middle class, as represented by the National Urban League—of the FWP: not only would it help record and preserve African American history and culture more faithfully, it would also employ African Americans in high-status positions in "the white collar field." Brown used much the same argument in another letter later that year to T. Arnold Hill, another National Urban League official: "The Negro has been so unfairly represented on the white collar projects, that I feel some such action is imperative. These young people should not lose their jobs. They have learned research and editorial techniques, and many have learned more about writing than any college can teach them. They tell me this experience has been educational for them. For them to be deprived of self-respecting and partly creative work now would be an injustice." The "self-respecting and partly creative work" that Brown wanted to vouchsafe to black white-collar workers was implicitly contrasted to his own writing, which his administrative tasks deferred and delayed interminably: "I think you realize that I am not asking for my own job. The sooner I get off the project, the sooner I'll get my long due novel finished. But I don't want all I've done to be wasted."[39]

As Brown suggests, the work that the FWP called on him and other African American writers, editors, and researchers to perform was only "partly creative." Carmody emphasizes Brown's orthographical labor in the transcription of the Slave Narrative Collection interviews, noting that he sent "state and local branches [of the FWP] a page-long list of proper spellings and a set of general guidelines."[40] But Brown also played an equally important administrative role. Although he did write prose essays for the American Guide series—one of which, "The Negro in Washington," is today considered a classic of its genre—the bulk of his work for the project proved to be strictly managerial, involving such mundane matters as travel reimbursements, understaffing, tensions surrounding the racial integration of the project's workforce, the selection of photographs, and a protracted series of conflicts over the proper division of labor between researchers and supervisors. A preliminary inspection of the archives relating to Brown's FWP work shows his involvement in a complex web of affiliations, hierarchies, and conflicting loyalties and the many frustrations he encountered as he tried to navigate this web.

Part of Brown's job, for example, was to oversee researchers who were actively engaged in the fieldwork that he, owing to his responsibilities as a college professor, could not conduct himself. All the one-on-one encounters with the Big Boys of the world would have to be farmed out to dozens of trained operatives, and it was Brown's job to instruct them, from a distance, in proper anthropological procedure. (Brown was not a trained anthropologist, but apparently he was close enough for the FWP.) "I hastily approve your going to the rural sections and not to books," he wrote in October 1936 to J. H. Harmon, a researcher who had coauthored a book titled *The Negro as a Business Man.* "[Books] might serve as guides to procedure. But a sympathetic approach to the people, which means no condescension and marked curiosity, should help even more."[41]

Brown's emphasis on sympathy for the ethnographic subject and the importance of qualitative fieldwork was balanced by a countervailing bureaucratic tendency within the FWP to conduct as much of the research on paper, away from the field, as possible. "What I want to know is this: am I doing the right thing with this material?" Brown's graduate student Ulysses Lee, whom he had hired as a researcher on the Washington, D.C., project, asks him in a letter of June 30, 1936:

> Mr. Braxton wants me to change to cataloguing statistics on the number of slaves sold in the District of Columbia. . . . Of course there would be less work in lifting those statistics from the files of the Library of Congress but, I thought, that the division of labor in this office would be such that Miss Roberts would do the library research while I would go hiking over fields (and the fields of Brightwood and the hills of Burville are no grassy meadows). I could, of course, send bulkier packages working at the library and I would eliminate all danger of sun-

stroke but, meanwhile Mrs. Patterson (a delightful old lady with a throaty giggle who has promised to tell me about downtown Vinegar Hill) could die and Vinegar Hill could die with her. Perhaps I've put too much stress on the experiences of the people themselves but, I think, it is more nearly possible to get an idea of the economic and social history of Washington Negroes from casual conversations with these old people than from a rhapsody in figures. Maybe I'm wrong but if I am, I know where to find the figures whereas, two weeks from today, I may not know where to find any one of the old people to whom I now have introductions.[42]

The ethical responsibility that African American intellectuals felt toward the life histories of the people they were interviewing inevitably clashed with the administrative protocols of data collection advocated by the government. The contrast between fieldwork and white-collar work (or, in another register, qualitative and quantitative methodologies) here takes the form of a racialized division of labor in which Lee sees his research role as primarily that of a fieldworker literally "hiking over the fields" to gather evidence of "the experiences of the people themselves," while the (presumably white) Miss Roberts does "the library research," composing a "rhapsody in figures." (This last figure of speech may be an echo of George Gershwin's 1924 *Rhapsody in Blue*, another white appropriation of black culture in a more "sophisticated" form.)

Lee's complaint about the sterility of statistics and "literary critiques" gains force from the fact that almost all the administrative personnel on the FWP were white. As Carmody notes, the FWP "took over work that had been started by black anthropologists and graduate students in the late 1920s and by the Federal Emergency Relief Administration (FERA) in the early 30s, employing black college students. . . . The administrative transition to the FWP . . . brought about several important changes, not the least of which was the shift in staff and leadership from the hands of black academics, college graduates, and graduate students into the hands of white government bureaucrats and white relief workers. . . . What began as a black initiative aimed at reexamining and reclaiming the history of slavery became a white-led project of national consolidation."[43] In such a situation, it seems inevitable that racial tensions would arise between the white government bureaucrats and the relatively few African American researchers who remained on the payroll, and it often fell to Brown to manage these conflicts.

One bureaucratic drama is especially worth recounting in the context of my earlier discussion of literary autonomy and sacrifice. The ideological struggle over control of the Virginia field guide gradually expands to one involving authorship or, more specifically, credit. Brown had not joined the FWP expecting to assert his rights as an author, and the prospect of the Virginia material's publication in book form was apparently first introduced by Henry Alsberg after the project was already under way. (It would ultimately appear, in 1940, as *The Negro in Virginia*.) "Alsberg wants some guarantee that the product of this new project should not be cast upon the Virginia broomsedge, but that it stands a reasonable chance for publication," Brown wrote to Roscoe Lewis, the "Negro unit supervisor" for the Virginia research, in September 1936. "I told him that I had not known of such an eventuality, that my greatest concern had been to get Negro material collected and Negro workers employed. I am to talk to him today about this publishing end."[44]

The possibility that the Virginia research would result in a published book seems to have engendered first a burgeoning literary pride ("Your job is the best one I've ever had," Lewis wrote to Brown on October 20, 1937; "I do think we are really getting along on a book. . . . It's really beginning to take shape") and subsequently a great anxiety. In his correspondence with Brown, Lewis complains about being consistently excluded from editorial decisions by his supervisor, Eudora Richardson. In a long, undated letter, most likely from 1937, he complains that Richardson had added "a summarizing paragraph apologizing for the ex-slave testimony" and that "she made it perfectly plain that I have nothing to do with the book now that my task of 'collecting material' is completed." The racialized division of labor described by Ulysses Lee recurs, with the black fieldworker "collecting material" and the white woman handling the more properly white-collar clerical work of collation and compilation.

It is possible, of course, to see Lewis's frustration as arising not from institutionalized racism but from the larger artistic philosophy of the New Deal itself, which, in Michael Szalay's account, viewed art making "not [as] a system of commodities at all, but [as] an administratively coordinated process of production." In an ideal situation, Szalay writes, "there would be no literary artifact the demand for which the state needed to enhance; instead, art would become an entirely procedural activity." The fact that actual finished books resulted from this "administratively coordinated process of production" was beside the point: "Producing 'books' was most assuredly not a 'necessity' . . . when writers were paid for their efforts. . . . Offering a wage for the labor of creation, but no dividends from an artifact over whose marketing and consumption a worker had no control and for which he or she was never cited as author, the Federal Writers' Project assimilated working-class politics, wage labor, and a performative aesthetic each to the other."[45] The FWP thus asked writers to trade literary autonomy—an often abstract concept made concrete, in this case, by the moral and legal rights conventionally associated with authorship—in exchange for a wage. One could write and be paid for writing in return for giving up both choice of subject and control over the ultimate fate of one's work.

But the literary impulse toward autonomy proved difficult to suppress completely, despite the best efforts of Eudora Richardson and other WPA functionaries. If one reads through the correspondence, it becomes clear that the investment of African American FWP employees like Brown, Lewis, and Lee in their projects was clearly authorial, as well as political. "Now that it appears that a book is going to be published, there crop up in my mind a dozen changes I wish to make almost every day," Lewis writes to Brown in a long, undated letter from the late 1930s. "I'm going to make a determined effort to get hold of a copy of the proof so that I can find out what is in the book. Also I imagine I'm going to have to buy a copy." To the injury of his exclusion from the editorial process—his marginalization as producer—was added the imagined insult of having to purchase a copy of the final product and thus being further reduced to the status of mere consumer.

Here the difference between "self-respecting and partly creative" white-collar work and the wholly creative, even more dignified work of literary authorship becomes clear. Lewis knew that he should not expect that his labor entitled to him to any benefits or privileges beyond the contractual wage the project paid him. But the dignity of authorship was not so easily renounced, especially when the theme of the text—the reality of African American life in the Jim Crow state of Virginia—was one so close to the writer's heart. "Its just a Goddam shame," he complains to Brown later in the same letter. "Just when I had begun to think that the book was a book she chops the hell out of it, three times in the last ten months. . . . Well, the way I feel, the hell with the project and with Eudora." No sooner has Lewis "begun to think that the book was a book"—that is, a work of art or literature, with some of the autonomous formal qualities that category implies—than its status as a purely bureaucratic make-work project is reasserted. Lewis reacts to this reassertion of the real purpose of the Virginia guide with disgust: "Sometimes I feel that I don't want a goddamned thing to do with this book. In many respects it is not what I wrote, and whatever 'credit' comes as a result of it, she can have. Frankly, I'm ashamed of it in its present form, though I admit I haven't seen its present form."[46]

It was Brown's job as administrator to manage the expectations of fieldworkers that they might have some substantial influence on the finished product, and his reply begins with an attempt to assuage Lewis's hurt pride with practicality and humor: "Take it easy, Greasy, you've got a long way to slide."[47] Nevertheless, by March 1939, Lewis's frustration has given way to complete disenchantment:

> I had just returned from Richmond feeling very miserable after seeing what Mrs. Richardson had done to my article on the Negro for the Guide. . . . Its [*sic*] a long story. I've been cutting and cutting and inserting and inserting. Got it down finally to 7500 words and she said it would have to come down to 5000. . . . She cuts out the sentence about mulattoes in the big house but retains the one about Mammies—I was a fool to put

it in, I realize now. And, in cutting, she has taken out all the life of the article, if there was any there. I hate to bother you about this but I presume it is coming to you and I want you to know that its not my essay any longer.[48]

Brown's remit as editor of Negro affairs was to keep the "life" in the field guides and the Slave Narrative Collection by guarding against the inclusion of pernicious racial stereotypes (such as "Mammies") and safeguarding the texts' anthropological authenticity. But the political and historical concern for authenticity was easily conflated with the aesthetic desire for autonomy: Lewis first referred to the chapter explicitly as "my article" before declaring ruefully that "its not my essay any longer." What is the central issue here? Is it fidelity to the historical reality of African American experience (the accurate observation of a phenomenon like "mulattoes in the big house")? Or is it the present-day African American fieldworker's (Lewis's) lack of control over his own work? The field guide archives reveal that these concerns are consistently interlinked, and it fell to Brown to adjudicate them.

෴ ෴ ෴

The story of Lewis's and, to a lesser extent, Brown's alienation from the products of their collective labor seems to call for a classical Marxist analysis. It is thus bitterly ironic that one of the crucial sticking points—the lack of proper credit for Lewis, Brown, and other African American contributors to the guide project—was justified, at least in part, by recourse to the collectivist, communitarian spirit favored by the WPA in general. "Confidentially about the by-line," Brown wrote to Lewis in September 1939. "I mentioned it to Newsom as a foregone conclusion, was startled to hear his unreadiness. Said the Project was supposed to be cooperative. I said it was your book. He said all these books are one-man jobs really, but that the boys on Capitol Hill and on the Project object like hell to single name books."[49] The WPA's desire to project an undifferentiated image of a seamless, nonegoistic, cooperative society resulted in the government's failure to acknowledge the contributions of some of that society's most disadvantaged and underrepresented citizens.

The contrast with MacLeish's notion of "intellectual office" could not be starker: whereas for him the poet-critic's sacrifice to the state was a mark of public honor, here the writer's sacrifice is accepted but not acknowledged, unknown to all but the workers themselves.

This was a strange, but not altogether unfamiliar, kind of exploitation: it was not the first time the U.S. government had enlisted the help of blacks and then failed to credit them. Brown and Lewis, like many African American intellectuals of the time, dealt with their sense of disappointment and disillusionment by reaffirming the bonds of friendship and solidarity between them, a connection that was only strengthened by the heartbreaking compromises each was making with the government. In a 1939 letter Brown teases Lewis about his developing fluency in bureaucratese: "Received your stuff shirt letter. . . . You oughta be ashamed. . . . I'm using parts of the letter as an example of Negro achievement (not of fooling the white folks)—and because it makes my office look as if its accomplishing something, getting letters like this."[50] Here Lewis's facility with the language of white-collar "white folks" is made a point of ironic pride, "an example of Negro achievement."

But in subsequent correspondence an undertone of deeper alienation intrudes as the two black white-collar workers, navigating their way together through an ocean of red tape, slips more and more into the old language of the plantation. "The biggest thing which bothers me is to have you worry about the thing after you have left it," Lewis had written to Brown in September 1937, when the latter was briefly considering leaving the project. "I'd hate to have you feel that you need to still run things through me— anticipate shipwreck, straighten me out. If its going to disturb your peace of mind you'd better let Alsberg get a big nigger for the job."[51] Brown, too, implicitly compares their bureaucratic superiors to slave masters: "In the chaotic upturning of the project here—being ordered to move, being ordered to stay, to move, to jump out, to jump back, honey, jump back—one chapter got away from me— 'Labor'—but I had the carbon you left with me and it was legible enough."[52]

The disjunction between the flat, colorless language of government bureaucracy and the more pungent lingo of Southern racism is highlighted in a remarkable memorandum Brown sent to Lewis shortly after he was reinstated as editor of Negro affairs:

Approved: Florence Kerr
Read by: Bumpley in Richmond Office
Dictated but not read: Sterling Brown
    (Editor on Nigger Affairs)
Read but not understood: T. C. Walker
    (Nigger in charge of the W.P.A.)
Dictator but not Red: Martin Dies

This is my first official letter. I'm back on the payroll. Damn, I sho' needs to be. Damn. It sho' took <u>time.</u>

I don't see why you're singing the blues about the essay. If all gets in that Eudora sent up it's the best N__ (Afro usage) essay we've ever had. After all this is a Virginia book, not one of "our group." Peace.

You've done a job in that essay that shakes from my back a whole heap of history Ph.D's and English majors. It's a good and valuable job. Peace.[53]

Brown's letter is a small masterpiece of the art of signifying, mixing together the modes of bureaucratic communication ("Dictated but not read," the mock-scholarly notation of "Afro usage") with that of African American vernacular ("singing the blues," "Peace") and leftist bonhomie ("Dictator but not Red"—Martin Dies was the senator who had accused the FWP, and Brown directly, of Communist ties). Although Lewis's essay is figured in emancipatory terms—it "shakes from [Brown's] back" the burden of poor academic scholarship on African American folk culture—their shared political project is also relentlessly ironized, as if to indicate that whatever pride they might have taken in it must be tempered by an awareness that the book, in the end, wouldn't really represent "our group." The memo is playful, angry, and tender all at the same time, a kind of poem in itself.

But the poetry of bureaucracy, however ingenious, is not a mode that is ever going to satisfy those who, not unreasonably, expect more from their government than unevenly distributed relief and minor concessions to cultural dignity. The art that Brown excelled in was the art of administration, which, like politics, is an art of the possible: it favors those who bend, who barter, who compromise. Compromise was a given in the relations between modernist poet-critics and the state, highlighted in high-minded appeals like MacLeish's "The Irresponsibles," which presented it as a duty that all writers and scholars shared equally. But we shouldn't forget that some writers had to compromise more than others, and that, in doing so, they exposed themselves to damaging accusations of complicity.

Brown was aware of such charges and gave one response to them in his 1944 call to arms (literally; it was meant to persuade African Americans to enlist, once again, to fight a war that many of them felt no connection to), "Count Us In": "What segregationists denounce as 'wanting to be with white folks,' Negroes think of as participating in the duties and enjoying the privileges of democracy. This means being with white folks, undoubtedly, since whites have nearly monopolized these duties and privileges. But it means being with them in fields and factories, in the armed forces, at the voting booths, in schools and colleges, in all the areas of service to democracy."[54] That Brown, in this stirring defense of public service, specifically mentions "fields and factories"—the two sites of the African American worker's most rigorous exploitation—may strike some radicals as a terrible irony. It was an irony he was willing to live.

5

The Foundations of Criticism

In 1945, R. P. Blackmur published a short essay in the *Sewanee Review* titled "The Economy of the American Writer." The piece was something of a departure for Blackmur, who had made his name as a close reader of texts rather than a social critic. Nonetheless, here we have Blackmur the close reader trying his hand at cultural criticism, beginning with a quotation from no less a master of the form than Alexis de Tocqueville: "Democracy not only infuses a taste for letters among the trading classes, but introduces a trading spirit into literature."[1] This "trading spirit," in Blackmur's estimation, had never been stronger in the United States than it was at the dawn of the postwar era, nor had there ever been more men and women of letters looking to sell their wares. He calls attention to the census of 1940, in which "some 11,806 persons reported themselves as professional authors, and some 44,000 additional reported as editors and reporters," noting that "even in a society so populous as ours, there cannot possibly be, unless the creative ability of man should profoundly change, 11,806 professional authors, and if there were they could not possibly be read. A few hundred good authors of all kinds—a half dozen great authors of any kind—would be the greatest stroke of luck plausible."[2]

What the United States had, Blackmur claimed, was not a great literary culture but an asymmetrical literary market, oversaturated with producers but poor in consumers, in which the good and the great competed for resources and attention with the mediocre and the delusional. The increase in general literacy had inevitably had powerful transformative effects on the world of literature, but these effects, to his mind, had never been guided or checked by any reliable institutional oversight. "The trade of writing is the chief positive obstacle, in our world, to the preservation and creation of the art of literature," Blackmur writes, "and it is an obstacle all the harder to overcome because there is a greater and negative obstacle, which goes with it, in the absence, through all our societies, of any social, public, or quasi-public institution which consistently and continuously encourages the serious writer to do his best work."[3] In the postwar period, Blackmur saw, "the art of literature"—which, for him and his cohort, meant first and foremost the underrecognized, unfinished project of modernism—would require institutional oversight and support on a scale unprecedented in American literary history.

For decades, as we have seen, a culture of literary and artistic experimentation had been sustained by the goodwill of a few wealthy patrons. In the first half of the twentieth century, Anglo-American literary modernism, threatened with the hostility and indifference of a growing mass public, adopted the temporary solution of packaging itself as a luxury commodity in order to compete in a market increasingly dominated by popular culture. Blackmur may have had something like this half measure in mind when he complains that even the nation's existing literary institutions merely reflect the values imposed on American society as a whole by the market: "[The writer's] readers if he has any, and his institutions if he can find any, both seem to judge him by the standards of the market and neither by the standards of literature nor by those of the whole society."[4] Modernism had been spared immersion in the destructive element of open competition, but only at the cost of being transformed into a luxury for a moneyed coterie. It had, in other words, not escaped the logic of the market but merely opted for a smaller, less competitive one.

Aristocratic patronage had been the way of modernism's formative decades, but Blackmur now had something different in mind. The precedent of the Works Progress Administration—for which Blackmur and his wife Helen had both worked—had emboldened

American intellectuals to feel that they could finally make the case to nonbohemians for the deliberate perpetuation of the support of serious literature as a social good. Moreover, modernism's assumption that it could come to some kind of working compromise with capitalism had been shaken by the Depression. "The theory of a cultural market does not work," Blackmur asserts:

> The market system of open competition does not work at all from the point of view of our presumed over-all social aim: the fostering and evaluation of the serious arts and the discouragement and devaluation of, not the frivolous, but the plain bad arts. . . . The market system as it affects writers is very much like the market system as it affects society as a whole; it dissolves all but the lowest values and preserves only the cheapest values: those which can be satisfactorily translated into money. . . . In the market system the automatic adjustment of economic value under free competition is supposed to take care of all the human values which make economic value significant, and it is supposed to do so by natural law.[5]

This antilibertarian attitude is fully consistent with what Szalay has described as "New Deal Modernism" and would seem to point to a Keynesian solution in which the state intervenes in the market in order to ensure its healthy functioning.[6] Yet Blackmur is conspicuously silent on the subject of state support for the arts in "The Economy of the American Writer." Perhaps surprisingly, his preferred solution to this problem of the interaction of the market and literature is not government interference—he in fact goes out of his way to disparage the Soviet system, which he finds no more conducive to aesthetic values than the American one—but a more carefully and expertly managed capitalism. The capitalist system had not been especially beneficial to literary values up to this point, Blackmur concedes, largely because of the laissez-faire character of Gilded Age industrialization: "Our society has been administered more by the forward drive of its inertia in the mass, which happened to be accelerating and therefore kept ahead of its problems, than it was administered by direct intelligence and imagination."[7] But capitalism, it was possible to believe in 1945, had been forever changed by the shocks of the Depression and the two world wars, and perhaps, in the postwar era, it would be possible to harness its formidable power in ways that would benefit the spread of serious literature.

But what corporate entities would allow for literary administration on this awesome scale? Blackmur put forward two "existing institutions which show potential aesthetic bias—the universities and the Foundations." "Must not all serious artists . . . grasp, both for their livelihood and for anchorage for their art, at any institutions, no matter how otherwise unlikely, that remove their values from the market?" he asks. Blackmur's rhetorical question is a little disingenuous; at least, he had already answered it for himself in the affirmative. At the time of his essay's publication, Blackmur had been teaching at Princeton for five years, and the essay grew out of a report for the Rockefeller Foundation. It is important to note, though, that in "The Economy of the American Writer" Blackmur voices important reservations about academia as well as the market: "In this country writers and artists have for some years been penetrating the universities; but it is too soon to tell with what results. The risk in the experiment is that the universities are themselves increasingly becoming social and technical service stations—are increasingly, that is, attracted into the orbit of the market system."[8] Whereas other modernist poet-critics like John Crowe Ransom tended to see the university as a city of refuge from the terrors of American capitalism, Blackmur keenly perceived the academy's crucial relation to the national labor market as a whole. The risk, as he saw it, was that universities, while employing poets and critics as teachers and thus keeping them from having to debase their work by adjusting its value to the fluctuations of the market (i.e., by selling it), would reintroduce market values into literature by virtue of the university's unacknowledged function as a "social and technical service station"—that is, a training ground for the professional-managerial class. This, for Blackmur, would be missing the point of the academy's sponsorship of modernism, protecting literature from one market (the market for literary commodities) by yoking it to another (the market for skilled labor). Blackmur concluded the essay with a warning that "the universities will need the courage as well as the judgment to see how vitally implicated are their own standards in the experiment. All's Alexandrian else."[9]

~~~

The philanthropic foundation, on the other hand, appeared to Blackmur to present a genuine alternative to the free-market system. It is important to note that at the time of the publication of "The Economy of the American Writer," foundations were still a relatively novel historical phenomenon; its author could easily remember a time before they existed at all. Foundations were the central institution of the nonprofit sector that emerged in the United States in the interwar period, which the economic historian Olivier Zunz has described as "the outcome of [a] unique encounter between philanthropy and the state. [The nonprofit sector] is a hybrid capitalist creation that operates tax free so long as profits are reinvested in the common good . . . [and] otherwise . . . retains many of the characteristics of for-profit enterprises."[10] Zunz calls foundations "a genuine American invention" and calculates that the number of philanthropic foundations in the United States grew from 27 in 1915 to 1,488 by 1955.[11] The growth of foundations can be linked, in part, to revisions of the tax code: the Rockefeller Foundation was chartered in the same year as the creation of the national income tax in 1913.[12] In 1936 the Ford Foundation was incorporated in response to the federal government raising the estate tax to 70 percent, the highest in the nation's history.[13]

These foundations differed from the family-controlled trusts of previous generations. Because they were obliged, in order to qualify for tax exemption, to serve the public good, their agendas tended to be broader than those of the trusts, which often catered to their founders' pet causes. They were also more scientific in their operation: to demonstrate their contribution to the public good in order to qualify for tax exemption, they had to proceed with a new methodological rigor. By the end of World War II, philanthropists had come to see themselves as major actors in the technocratic reorganization of American society. "Foundations," the journalist Mark Dowie wrote in *American Foundations: An Investigative History*, "have historically seen their function as the identification of root causes rather than outright charity," and their activities thus took on a diagnostic as well as a strictly philanthropic function.[14] "Characteristic of the new foundations was their recruiting of experts to conduct in-house investigations as well as to promote different educational and professional programs," Zunz writes. "Foundation managers developed connections within the larger world of expertise from which they could recruit, and on which they could always call."[15] It is hardly surprising that poet-critics, having already been prevailed on to edit magazines, teach college courses, and act as government bureaucrats, would be among the experts that philanthropic foundations began to court.

Blackmur's philanthropic career grew out of his youthful friendship with John Marshall, the associate director of the Rockefeller Foundation's Humanities Division. Marshall and Blackmur had known each other since their adolescent years in Cambridge, Massachusetts, in the early 1920s, when the former was an undergraduate at Harvard and the latter the proprietor of Dunster House, a bookstore that was a hub for Cambridge literary life. Even before the war, Marshall had been exploring new ways of subsidizing literary culture in the United States. Since its inception in 1913, the foundation had funded major national and international projects in medicine, public health, and rural and agricultural education. In common with the other big American philanthropies, the Rockefeller Foundation had historically put the bulk of its energies and assets into scientific research, including research into the military and national defense; from the 1930s onward, it had also been a crucial player in the development of the social sciences. The foundation's support for the arts and humanities, by contrast, was comparatively underdeveloped; the funding it did provide for the humanities tended to take the form of grants to established academic institutions in support of traditional scholarly disciplines like archaeology and classical philology.[16] The Rockefeller Foundation functioned as a supplement to the administrative budgets of elite American universities but did little to actively shape the institutional culture of the humanities in the way it did that of the natural and social sciences.

By the mid-1930s, however, this conservative, academic approach toward arts funding was beginning to change. Marshall's arrival at the foundation in 1933 coincided with a larger move, under the directorship of David H. Stevens, away from the accumulation of traditional scholarship and toward the democratic goal of wide public dissemination of culture.[17] In an attempt to shift the focus of his philanthropic attention from the academy to the public, Marshall turned to Blackmur, who served as the foundation's resident literary expert in much the same way in which prominent social scientists like Harold Lasswell and Paul Lazarsfeld had served as communications experts before and during the war.[18] In keeping with Marshall's focus on the public sphere rather than academia, the institution toward which Blackmur first directed the Rockefeller Foundation's philanthropic attention was not the university but the little magazine. By the mid-1940s, the twilight of the age of modernist little magazine seemed to be approaching. Legendary magazines like the *Dial*, the *Little Review, Hound and Horn*, and the *Criterion* had all ceased publication, victims of the disastrous effects of the Depression on the economy and of the shifting focus of their core readership away from art and literature and toward politics and the war effort. They had been replaced by a few new publications—among them *Partisan Review* (founded in 1934), the *Kenyon Review* (1939), and the *Sewanee Review* (established in the 1890s but revitalized in the 1940s under the editorship of Allen Tate)—which were prestigious but financially unstable. By the mid-1940s the rapid growth and potentially leveling effects of postwar consumer culture were already obvious to most American literary intellectuals, and the little magazine's days appeared to be numbered.

Blackmur began by enlisting two veterans of the American little-magazine scene, Malcolm Cowley and Lionel Trilling, to the cause. On September 18, 1946, Marshall informed his superiors that Blackmur, Cowley, and Trilling were assembling "a larger panel" of experts to "recommend a list of not more than eight magazines which they regarded as worthy of RF assistance." The selection process was to be a matter of private deliberation, not public debate; Marshall specified that "this small panel would be protected throughout by remaining unidentified and it would probably be desirable that even the larger panel should not in any way be announced." The foundation's financial support to the little magazines would not be massive, but it would be enough to allow them to raise the level of payment for their contributors: "as suggested by Blackmur, $7.50 for a page of 300 words of prose, $10.00 for a comparable page of verse."[19]

In October 1946 Blackmur drafted letters cosigned by Cowley, Trilling, and himself to many of the most prominent literary figures in the United States, including the poet-critics W. H. Auden, Louise Bogan, Kenneth Burke, Randall Jarrell, Marianne Moore, Wallace Stevens, Robert Penn Warren, Yvor Winters, and William Carlos Williams. "For reasons that will later become apparent," the letters begin, "we should be very grateful for your best opinion as to what literary magazines now being published in the United States are of the most use to literature. . . . On the safe assumption that literary magazines like these always need money and that their contributors are always paid too little, if at all, the object of our question is, first, to take advice as to what existing magazines most deserve such help and, on their record, why; and second, to devise methods of obtaining and distributing such help." Blackmur goes on to specify four criteria to bear in mind with regard to a little magazine's quality: "Introduction of new writers; Support of talented writers, young and older; Maintaining of critical standards; Interest in the other arts and in society." The letters end on a note of considerable urgency: "Our interest in what you may have to say could not be more serious or more immediate. In short, we are writing to you in the belief that, with your aid, genuine action might shortly become possible toward the consistent support of several literary magazines. Certainly any effort, not plainly futile, is worth making."[20]

Blackmur's intention was thus both to compile a list of potential grantees and to gather suggestions about how support could be best administered. This kind of survey of the American literary intelligentsia wasn't entirely unprecedented; the format in certain respects resembled symposia conducted by the little magazines themselves, such as the "The Situation in American Writing," which the *Partisan Review* had published in 1939. However, the flat bureaucratic tone of the letter and the fact that it made no mention of any future publication of the survey's results led many of the writers contacted to give exceptionally candid responses. A few acknowledged the unusual secrecy of the survey (Edmund Wilson refers to "your mysterious letter," and Eric Bentley calls it "nothing if not cryptic"), but it seems to have been generally understood that some kind of philanthropic support was involved, quite possibly because Blackmur's friends in literary circles already knew of his links to Marshall and the Rockefeller Foundation at this point.[21]

Unsurprisingly, most of the respondents were eager to declare their enthusiasm and support for the foundation's grand undertaking. "Delighted to get your letter this morning and to know that some movement is under way to help the magazines in this country that really care about literature," Alfred Kazin wrote, and F. O. Matthiessen concurred that "any coherent plan of subsidy for these or similar magazines would have unmistakably profound value for our culture." Robert Penn Warren was equally favorable: "If you all can see that some money gets turned into the little magazines, I shall applaud. I think the country would be a lot poorer without them." "I think your suggestion is a very good one indeed," Kenneth Burke wrote, "and if carried out, it might well have quite a startling effect. At least, there is much to be gained by subsidizing serious literature. And there is much to be gained by finding new ways of doing so (ways that will have a certain jolt value). The same sums, expended in the usual ways, would [probably have] a less stimulating effect than if thus suddenly presented."[22]

More interesting and revealing, however, are the critiques of the proposed project, almost all of which, notably, came from poet-critics as opposed to academic scholars (who were more unreservedly enthusiastic). One predictable point of controversy in these early years of the Cold War was the leftist political orientation of *Partisan Review*, which had originally aligned itself with the American Communist Party and, by the mid-1940s, was still associated with a heterodox anti-Stalinist Trotskyism. Marianne Moore's short response is mostly taken up with registering the fact that she "strongly disliked the propagandist period of PARTISAN REVIEW (I have not seen more than one or two issues since that time)."[23] One may assume that Moore, an outspoken proponent of American patriotism during World War II (and, as we have seen, an inveterate antagonist of agonism), objected to the *Partisan Review*'s antinationalist position during the war. But even those respondents closer to its ideological position expressed reservations about the magazine's politics. Randall Jarrell, for instance, responding on *Nation* stationery, voices a representative suspicion of the intermingling of aesthetics and politics in the little magazine: "Although its politics are doctrinaire and academic in that funny New York professional-left way, they haven't prevented it from printing other groups, Stalinists excepted. It's an awfully shrewd, professional, competent magazine, so far as the editing is concerned. The worst things about it are its extraordinary limitations and lack of imagination: everything is looked at from the point of view of someone who's semi-Marxist, fairly avant-garde, reasonably Bohemian, anti-bourgeois, cosmopolitan, anti-Stalinist, lives in New York, likes Mondrian, etc., etc., etc." Jarrell's primary objection to the magazine's "professional-left" orientation is not its potential political influence but its distortion of the existing literary field: *Partisan Review*'s politics were objectionable not in themselves but because they imposed a limitation of perspective and an overrepresentation of a particular group of writers and critics. Indeed, as Jarrell continues his critique, it becomes clear that the problem is not so much ideology as it is favoritism: "*Partisan* itself is too much of a movement: the editors will print bad things by 'our' people that they wouldn't consider from outsiders—take Paul Goodman, take Elizabeth Hardwick's story about [Paul] Tillich, etc." Jarrell contrasts this literary cronyism with an ideal of perfect editorial disinterestedness, which he associates, like Eliot before him, with those who are or had been practicing artists or writers themselves: "A thoroughly good magazine would require editors who like things simply because they're good; people who care for intrinsic values first of all, and who understand better—either because of memory or because of imagination—what it's like to make a work of art."[24]

The ever-outspoken William Carlos Williams takes an even harder line on the subject of ideology, lumping what he calls the "big three" magazines together and likening them—somewhat improbably, given the vehement anti-Stalinism of American intellectual culture at the time—to organs of Soviet propaganda: "To hell with them all with their scholarly editors each with his prejudices and predilections, *Kenyon, Sewanee* and *Partisan:* each with some sort of axe to grind. To me that is beyond the field of the arts, this side of the field of the arts. . . . All the little magazines today seem small imitations of some Soviet-like direction implicit in their editorial policies."[25] For Williams, the scholarly and the political are equally pernicious in that they imply a direction of artistic energies toward certain predetermined ends; in each case, the editors have an axe to grind other than a desire to showcase and stimulate artistic production as it exists in its natural state. Presumably Williams would have favored an approach closer to that of 1920s-era little magazines like *Others* and *Contact* (he had been closely involved with both), which took a relatively hands-off approach to editorship. But although his response is clearly colored by nostalgia for the golden age of high modernism, Williams's use of the epithet "Soviet-like" suggests that the Cold War conjuncture is not irrelevant here. The respondents' widespread suspicion of political ideology was itself a kind of ideology, and their concern for pure, disinterested taste—for "intrinsic values" and an unmolested "field of the arts"—reflects a more general postwar distrust of large bureaucratic institutions, epitomized by the Soviet Communist state. Although the issue under discussion here is private philanthropic support and not government funding, many of the respondents appear distinctly uncomfortable with the idea of funding for the arts by a large bureaucratic organization. The fear of ideology and a "Soviet-like direction" displayed by Williams is in part a classically modernist gesture toward autonomy, but it is also a distinctly postwar fear of bureaucratic planning per se.

This uneasiness with bureaucracy helps explain why even respondents less committed to the modernist concept of autonomy than Williams do not imagine a bold new future for the little magazine in America but simply increased support for the market they already know. Although Jarrell and Williams's critiques are framed in the modernist language of aesthetic autonomy, they are compatible with a nascent postwar libertarianism founded on distrust of bureaucratic administration and faith in efficient markets. The libertarian economist Ludwig von Mises's polemic *Bureaucracy* had been published a couple of years before, and although nearly all the respondents to the Rockefeller survey were on the left side of the political spectrum, ideas about the inherent inefficiency and despotism of big bureaucratic institutions were becoming popular among liberals as well as conservatives during that period.

An unlikely representative of this kind of laissez-faire libertarian attitude is Auden, the former Communist, who proposes a kind of ratification of the literary economy that already exists. "As I see it, there ought to be three kinds of magazines," he writes:

> The real little mags, i.e. small mags [run] by little groups of intolerant eager young men who all think each other geniuses and pay each other almost nothing but get into print. Of these there should be as many as possible.
>
> The Middle magazines, like P. R. + Kenyon who select the promising writers from the first group. Here I think the important thing is to keep the number of such magazines down so that (a) the standard of any one is not lowered too much by competition + (b) Any capital available for such a venture is concentrated and they can afford to pay more for contributions which will keep the established writers with them a little longer.
>
> The Big magazines, e.g. New Yorker, Atlantic, Harpers, the fashion mags etc. which really have the big money. Here the important thing is ceaseless propaganda as their editorial policy to persuade them to take more "highbrow" stuff.[26]

In the mid-1940s it was widely assumed, and not only by Auden, that there would continue to be a thriving upscale market for serious poetry and fiction in big magazines like the *New Yorker,* and if the big magazines were going to continue to publish the best writers, then the little magazine was little more than a feeder or farm team for the bigger ones. In this sense, the perspectives expressed by many of the survey's respondents are uniformly, even classically conservative, oriented not toward radical change but toward the prudent consolidation of the status quo. The most important question is how to assure the continued existence of the good literature that already exists against the force of the market, not to alter existing arrangements so as to produce an entirely new and more equitable kind of literary society. (The contrast with the younger Auden, who felt sure that civilization was on the verge of a massive transformation and that writers would play an essential part in it, couldn't be starker.) Contrary to the pluralistic intentions of Marshall, there is less concern with democratization or expansion of the literary field than with preserving its current dimensions.

Such preservation does not necessarily entail an expansion of the field of little magazines (although this eventually happened, especially in the 1950s and 1960s, largely as a side effect of the expansion of the educational system and the falling costs of production associated with the so-called mimeograph revolution). It might even mean a winnowing of the field, with available resources being divided among only a few little magazines (the biggest, as it were), allowing them to corner the market on quality literature. To some respondents, even the reduced field of 1946 looked overcrowded; Matthiessen, for instance, complained that "new 'little magazines' are always being started with the result that now the danger is that too many of them cover the same ground and get in each other's way in point of circulation and chance for survival. It might well be more effective if there were fewer of them and those few with far greater subsidies."[27] Auden, too, was dubious about the value of the existing little magazines:

> To be quite frank, I can't read more than one or two contributions in any of the magazines you mention. They all start off well in the first few issues because all the fairly good writers rally round to give the editor (whom they usually know personally) a rousing send-off. After that they develop a cliquish cove of constant contributors and stray new arrivals. It is obvious that no magazine, let alone several competing ones, can keep up a really high standard because there simply isn't enough first-rate stuff available at their prices. The established writer is obviously going to sell his wares in the dearest market and once he has a name, the little magazines can't afford him.[28]

Although most of the respondents asserted that little magazines, in principle, should be protected, few of them relished the idea of there being any more of them than there already were, and some didn't care if there were any. Louise Bogan was the most dismissive of the overall project of reviving the glory days of the modernist little magazine, which she saw as a relic of a vanished interwar world:

> Let me begin by saying that I believe the little magazine in America, at the moment, is in a state of obsolescence. The whole literary situation which prevailed during the period when the little mag. flourished has changed to such an extent that new terms must be applied to new conditions. Publishers of the commercial kind are now so eager to get new writers of talent that they sign them up right out of the pages of the periodicals . . . in which they first appear. I do not think that any good poet appearing in America, just now, could fail to get some sort of appreciation, almost immediately. . . . The little magazine, therefore, now prints, almost exclusively, second-rate work.

There are shades here of MacLeish's contempt for "little books to lie on little tables," an impatience for good poetry to transcend the limited sphere of coteries and luxury editions and realize its true commercial potential. Although Bogan feels little sympathy for the "little," she did advocate a medium-sized magazine "of a serious yet readable and lively kind" modeled on Cyril Connolly's *Horizon*, which "demonstrate[s] how a kind of worldly, informed, and witty approach can bring new material into being, and give it an audience and a market." Bogan, then, unlike many of her fellow respondents, does imagine serious literature growing bigger in the sense of reaching more of the lay readers modernism had lost or abandoned. Her lack of interest in the little magazine is in part, no doubt, aesthetic, grounded in a general distaste for experimental literature: "The life has now gone out of rebellion and experiment as such, in literature. What we need is widening and deepening of a field already conquered."[29] Good American poetry, having been nurtured by the coterie-based economy of the modernist little magazine, is now finally in a position to compete in a wider literary market alongside other cultural products. Thus the little magazine appears as, at best, a sort of vestige of a previous stage in the evolution of

American literature; the goal should not be to preserve its former function of encouraging "experiment" but to "widen and deepen" the literary culture it has allowed to come into being.

Finally, it is fascinating to track the way in which the New Deal social democratic ethos that underlies Blackmur and company's concern for the autonomy of modernism—an ethos that held that the arts, like other public goods, must be supported and protected from the vagaries and depredations of the free market—confronts obstacles in the form of a mandarin aristocratic worldview that rejects the economization of the aesthetic entirely. Perhaps the most considered and provocative formulation of this perspective comes from Wallace Stevens, a poet-critic with more managerial experience than most. (He was, famously, vice president of an insurance company by day.) In the first of two letters written in response to Blackmur's inquiry, Stevens questions whether the proposed scheme of revitalizing the little magazines could even be realistically accomplished without astronomical amounts of capital: "Poetry as the beneficiary of a trust fund would require something like $1,000,000.00 to carry on. . . . Even with all this, Poetry would be a modest establishment. But no-one will write for it any longer for love. The New Republic would discover that it was the tool of the luxurious. Everyone would expect poets to buy the drinks, and so on." Stevens, as a sober insurance executive, is closely attentive to the bottom line here, but also, more interestingly, to the possible side effects of the private endowment of literature. He considers not merely whether the support for little magazines would be effective but also whether it might have unintended consequences that would transform literary culture beyond recognition. For Stevens, literary work is done, first and foremost, not for money but for love and, to adopt a word he uses frequently in his second letter, for "honor." The introduction of a financial motive—or even just the ability to make a viable living as a writer or editor—compromises the basic terms of the economy of art, making literature and the little magazines into a "tool of the luxurious" rather than a preserve of the domestic, aristocratic values of love and honor. Speaking as eloquently for the mandarins as Auden and Bogan had for the libertarians, Stevens concludes his first letter thus:

Let me wind the thing up for the present by saying that the objects in the attic of life never seemed dearer to me than now when I see the three of you approaching them with pots of gilding. I hope you won't think that I am not interested. Personally, I have a horror of the sort of thing that is done for money. That is about all there is nowadays. It has nothing whatever to do with what means anything to me nor, I believe, to you and the other two men who signed your letter.[30]

It is interesting that Stevens was the only respondent to consider how the motivation of writers and the constitution of literary culture might be affected by the introduction of private subsidy. Furthermore, he argues, not only might writers become greedy and self-interested, but also the infusion of large amounts of money would dramatically transform literature's fundamental relation to the public sphere: "It is clear enough that an adequate endowment of merely the better existing magazines would run into something fantastic. A lot of new things now suppressed might be looked for and [people] would talk about the privileged few, the social duty of the trustees, etc. A man with any money at all is beset with other people's plans for spending it." Stevens recognizes the danger of literature becoming beholden to a sense of "social duty"—a familiar modernist anxiety about the interaction of art with public culture, but stated here in terms of obligation rather than contamination or leveling. (We are back to MacLeish's position in "Invocation to the Social Muse": poets have a duty only to poetry.) For Stevens, this anxiety is commingled with more practical problems of administration: "Everyone whom you asked to contribute would know in advance that the universal practice in the administration of chests is to specialize in a group of donors. Who is going to contribute on such a scale to such a project? What special claim have literary men to such preference?" Presciently, Stevens suggests that in allying itself with the Rockefeller Foundation and other charitable institutions, literature is taking on the burden of having to justify itself, having to make a "special claim" for its preeminent cultural status, and not just to an amorphous public but to a small number of donors who possess the economic capital necessary to underwrite literary activity on this vast scale. Literature could perhaps become big without selling out to the market, but at the cost of making itself explicable, rationalizable, justifiable, accountable—an object, that is, of perpetual critique.

✥ ✥ ✥

In conclusion, we should consider the respondents' consistent emphasis on "criticism" and "critical standards," which was built into the Rockefeller survey from the start. Although publications like *Partisan Review*, the *Kenyon Review*, and the *Sewanee Review* regularly printed fiction and poetry, they were seen, first and foremost, as critical magazines. Their most important character-istics, for most of the survey's respondents, were their frequent publication of literary and cultural criticism and their mainte-nance of high aesthetic standards in their decisions about what to publish. But if the fundamental social problem under consider-ation was the use to literature, why support literature through little magazines at all? Why not fund publishers, bookstores, or lit-erary societies or even make monetary grants directly to writers, as Stevens tentatively suggests?[31] If the goal was to promote the health of American literature, why fund criticism rather than creative writing?

I have already suggested that poet-critics appealed to foundation officers like Marshall for the same reason that MacLeish appealed to Roosevelt, and academic poet-critics like Blackmur, Ransom, and Tate appealed to university administrators of the same period: in the unique compromise they embodied between the apparently antithetical values of charisma and bureaucracy, they were perfect management material. But supporting literary culture by soliciting its established experts had disadvantages. As self-interested agents worried about the decline and even the disappearance of literary culture, they had strong incentives to align themselves with institu-tions that sought, in Blackmur's words, to "remove their values from the market." And as social actors predisposed to view the preserva-tion of the existing state of poetic and literary culture as a public good, they were extremely adept at generating convincing justifica-tions for it.

This points to a long-standing dilemma in the study of philanthropic foundations as economic institutions. There is no way to
define "good"—in the sense of the common social good that philanthropy is meant to promote—as rigorously as economists can define
"value." Value, for classical economics, is created out of the market's
demand for commodities. The public good often (though not always) stands in opposition to the market's imperatives, but it is up to
philanthropists and philanthropic institutions to determine what
that good might be and how it might rationally be sought. In his
1962 paper "A Theory of Philanthropy," the economist Kenneth
Boulding wondered

> whether there is anything that might be called "rational" phil-
> anthropic behavior. What are the standards, in other words, by
> which we can judge whether a man, or a foundation, or even a
> government is giving away its money wisely. It is clear that in
> practice we do have some standards and it therefore must make
> some kind of sense to talk about rational philanthropy. Philan-
> thropic donations, that is to say, are not wholly random or arbi-
> trary. They are capable of criticism according to some welfare
> function even though the function may be very difficult to
> specify.[32]

Philanthropic organizations posed a problem for economic theory,
Boulding realized, because their actions could not be rationalized
according to a pure capitalist logic of profit maximization. The
foundation, in other words, was a big financial actor whose economic behavior could not be analyzed in the same way as the firm's
or even the state's (if the state's activity was viewed as oriented
toward the protection of its military and economic interests, at
least). Philanthropic donations still had to be "capable of criticism"—
indeed, their gifts were on such a tremendous scale that they de-
manded rational critical assessment—but they weren't subject to
the kinds of purely rational calculations economists were used to
making of purely capitalist, exchange-oriented institutions. "A
foundation," Boulding points out, "must make choices much as a
firm does. It has to decide that A is worthy and B is not. It must de-

velop a policy according to which it makes and, perhaps even more important, justifies its decisions. Even though its purpose is to do good rather than to make profits and even though profits have a certain objectivity of measurement which the good has not, nevertheless, it is presumably in the interest of a foundation to do more good in its own estimation rather than less."[33] Therefore, since philanthropic foundations are aiming at a maximization of good rather than a maximization of financial profit, they are in constant need of rationales, of justification.

And justification, as we have seen, is a service that critics have always been able to supply. The function of criticism, typically viewed as supplemental to art and literature, is not merely to judge and evaluate but also to justify and rationalize what otherwise risks appearing to be a totally irrational realm of autonomous values, accountable to no logic or authority but its own. Poet-critics, as mediators between that mysterious twilight realm of artistic creation and the daylight world of getting and spending, were perfectly placed to guide that effort. Since criticism had long been in the justification business, it was a natural fit for the grants economy perpetuated by big bureaucratic institutions like philanthropic foundations, universities, and (to a lesser extent) government agencies, which were subject to public scrutiny and needed clearly articulated rationales. Whereas in a purely market-driven expansion of the literary field, the big winners might simply be the "best" writers—that is, the most popular and commercially successful, those whose work was in highest demand, either by the general public or by the tastemakers and gatekeepers who happen to be in control of prestige magazines—this particular philanthropic form of growth privileged, above all others, the village explainers.

At the same time, the substantial critiques offered by Williams, Jarrell, and Stevens reflect a concern for the quality of poetic culture that could come only from practicing poets, from those who not only understood the values of the literary world but also lived them. They didn't simply will the continued existence of poetry under any circumstances; they wanted to preserve poetry's autonomous character, which included not just the formal properties of the texts or their mode of distribution but also the psychological motivations of the poets who produced them. (Think of Stevens's aristocratic "horror of those things that are done for money.") The double bind, then, is obvious: if exposure to administration and to finance is harmful to poetry's autonomous character, how can provision be made for its continued existence in a market society?

To put it another way: What role could foundations and universities possibly have to offer poet-critics but administration? This produces a terrible paradox, since administration is taken, on the one hand, to be antithetical to poetry and, on the other, to be its only salvation: there was a very real shared feeling that without support from foundations and universities, poetry would cease to exist. Note that none of the conscientious objections of the poet-critics who responded to Blackmur's survey involved turning down the foundation money completely. The stakes were too high for that, and beggars—even noble beggars—can't be choosers.

The solution was to let the choosers be the beggars. The wide agreement among the respondents on the positive social value of criticism—its value as a public good, but also its evaluability according to rational norms—made it easier to make a case for funding it, for justifying its existence. Even if none of the respondents to Blackmur's survey would claim that literary criticism was more valuable or important—and thus more deserving of funding—than poetry or fiction, there does seem to have been broad agreement that criticism, good and bad, was easier to come to consensus about, more inherently justifiable, than literature. The thinking seems to have been as follows: if you had to institutionalize something, institutionalize criticism because it was in greater danger than imaginative literature, and because the establishment and promulgation of sound standards would in turn inevitably produce better literature. Criticism thus stood to literature as the foundation stood to capitalism: both were ameliorative institutions checking the most destructive and antisocial tendencies of the larger, more protean force. Philanthropy would act as capitalism's conscience, and criticism would act as literature's; each was conceived as a kind of guide, or mentor, making sure that its charge didn't go too far or destroy itself.

We are beginning to see why literary criticism—which has never generated any appreciable economic value or credibly presented itself to the public as a discipline as rigorous as the sciences—benefited so handsomely from the long postwar technocratic boom. Our current culture of institutionalized criticism was born out of a collective realization that American literary culture would need to grow, but also a collective fear that that growth would be wild, unrestricted, and damaging to the literary intelligentsia of the prewar period and the aesthetic standards they had painstakingly developed over decades. As Williams put it in his letter to the Rockefeller Foundation, invoking another postwar discourse by a poet-critic (Walt Whitman's "Democratic Vistas"): "The vistas are limitless. But had damn well better be limited if any good is to be done."[34]

Conclusion: With the Program

IN THE SPRING OF 1946, W. H. Auden, by then resident in America for seven years and newly naturalized as a U.S. citizen, delivered the Phi Beta Kappa poem at Harvard University's commencement ceremony. This was the first Harvard class to graduate after the suspension of hostilities in September 1945, and Auden began by alluding to this watershed, as well as to the presence of returned soldiers on campus:

> Ares at last has quit the field,
> The bloodstains on the bushes yield
>   To seeping showers,
> And in their convalescent state
> The fractured towns associate
>   With summer flowers.
>
> Encamped upon the college plain
> Raw veterans already train
>   As freshman forces;
> Instructors with sarcastic tongue
> Shepherd the battle-weary young
>   Through basic courses.

The poem's opening is relatively reverent, as befits a ceremonial address at one of the nation's oldest and most prestigious private universities. But there is mischief afoot already in these opening stanzas. The reference, for example, to "raw veterans [training] as freshman forces," while explicitly designating the young soldiers admitted to Harvard on the GI Bill, also alludes to the rise of the New Criticism and its surprising popularity with American undergraduates. The double reference becomes clearer in the following lines:

> Among bewildering appliances
> For mastering the arts and sciences
>   They stroll or run,
> And nerves that steeled themselves to slaughter
> Are shot to pieces by the shorter
>   Poems of Donne.
>
> Professors back from secret missions
> Resume their proper eruditions,
>   Though some regret it;
> They liked their Dictaphones a lot,
> They met some big wheels, and do not
>   Let you forget it.

The subterranean connection between war and literary criticism that underlies Eliot's "Gerontion" is here elevated and exposed to the light: New Critical close reading (practiced, of course, on "the shorter poems of Donne," that old favorite of Eliot's) is, in its way, as psychologically harrowing as "slaughter." Students who have served as foot soldiers in the war against fascism are now taking out their aggression on the masterpieces of English literature, which prove, in some ways, to be a more formidable opponent. The professors, too, have been changed by their contributions to the war effort, which allowed them to briefly ascend to the dignity of civil servants with Dictaphones interacting with politicians and other "big wheels." In Auden's satirical reimagining, the campus is both a war zone and a pastoral idyll, a field of intellectual conflict and a green world distant from actual physical danger.

Having established the postwar academic setting, "Under Which Lyre" turns to its true subject: the contest, now that "Ares . . . has

quit the field," between two attitudes toward life and education represented by two other deities, Hermes and Apollo.

> Let Ares doze, that other war
> Is instantly declared once more
> 　　　　Twixt those who follow
> Precocious Hermes all the way
> And those who without qualms obey
> 　　　　Pompous Apollo.
>
> Brutal like all Olympic games,
> Though fought with smiles and Christian names
> 　　　　And less dramatic,
> This dialectic strife between
> The civil gods is just as mean,
> 　　　　And more fanatic.

Just as *The Orators'* second ode adapted the style of Pindar to celebrate a school rugby game, here Auden invokes an ancient ritual—the Olympic Games—to bring a heightened sense of drama to
this petty and essentially polite conflict, "fought with smiles and
Christian names." The two teams, in Auden's schema, are distinct:

> The sons of Hermes love to play
> And only do their best when they
> 　　　　Are told they oughtn't;
> Apollo's children never shrink
> From boring jobs but have to think
> 　　　　Their work important.

The sons of Hermes are playful and rebellious, while Apollo's children
are dutiful and a bit deluded. (It should already be obvious which side
Auden is on.) Over the course of the next ten stanzas, the qualities of
Apollo and his followers are described: he is power hungry ("He loves
to rule, has always done it"); unimaginative ("Unable to invent the
lyre,/[He] creates with simulated fire/Official art"); business minded
("He pays particular/Attention to Commercial Thought"); sporty

("Athletic, extrovert, and crude"); and bipartisan ("Today his arms, we must confess, / From Right to Left have met success").

In the poem's version of postwar American culture, Apollonianism is clearly the dominant force. "To him ascend the prize orations," Auden writes, harking back to his own "Address for a Prize-Day" and ironically signaling that he—a Hermetic poet—has somehow ended up doing an Apollonian's job. He leaves his sympathies unambiguous when he shifts, in the second half of the poem, to first-person plural:

> No matter; He shall be defied;
> White Aphrodite is on our side:
> What though his threat
> To organize us grow more critical?
> Zeus willing, we, the unpolitical,
> Shall beat him yet.
>
> Lone scholars, sniping from the walls
> Of learned periodicals,
> Our facts defend,
> Our intellectual marines,
> Landing in little magazines
> Capture a trend.

These stanzas mark a return to a trope Auden had mostly abandoned by the 1940s: the mock-heroic description of students and young people as spies or revolutionaries. Here it gets combined with the image of undergraduate soldiers from the poem's opening lines as Hermetic modernists are imagined as "intellectual marines / Landing in little magazines" and setting their sights on pompous, Apollonian "fat figures in the public eye."

The poem's final lines are its most frequently remembered and quoted. In them, Auden advises his charges to "keep well the Hermetic Decalogue, / Which runs as follows":

> Thou shalt not do as the dean pleases,
> Thou shalt not write thy doctor's thesis

On education,
Thou shalt not worship projects nor
Shalt thou or thine bow down before
          Administration.

Thou shalt not answer questionnaires
Or quizzes upon World-Affairs,
          Nor with compliance
Take any test. Thou shalt not sit
With statisticians nor commit
          A social science.

Thou shalt not be on friendly terms
With guys from advertising firms,
          Nor speak with such
As read the Bible for its prose,
Nor, above all, make love to those
          Who wash too much.

In these three stanzas, a new postwar cultural archetype is sketched. It is remarkable, in fact, how closely Auden's "sons of Hermes" resemble the ideal type of the college-educated, literary, mildly countercultural young person of the ensuing seven decades, even up to the present day. This person has experience of higher learning but is not in thrall to it ("Thou shalt not do as the dean pleases"); she resists the imperialist extension of social scientific data collection into everyday life ("Thou shalt not answer questionnaires"); she is anticapitalist or, at least, contemptuous of the overtly mercantile ("Thou shalt not be on friendly terms / With guys in advertising firms"); she is even already adopting some of the bohemian hygiene habits that will come to be associated with the hippie movement ("Nor, above all, make love to those / Who wash too much"). About the only detail Auden gets wrong is his assumption that the new generation of Hermetics would be Christians.

It's the final stanza, though, that most tellingly summarizes its author's attitude toward the new cultural economy that was then coming into being:

> Thou shalt not live within thy means
> Nor on plain water and raw greens.
> If thou must choose
> Between the chances, choose the odd;
> Read *The New Yorker*, trust in God;
> And take short views.[1]

Unsurprisingly, given the views he expressed in the Rockefeller survey conducted later the same year, Auden expects his Hermetic disciples to dabble in "learned periodicals" and "little magazines" but to treat the *New Yorker*—already, by 1946, the epitome of middlebrow liberal cultural consensus—as sacrosanct. "Under Which Lyre" presented one model for the new technocratic modernism. Its initiates would be of working- and middle-class backgrounds but trained in elite academic settings, which they would have accessed through some combination of merit and government assistance. They would be skeptical of the cult of higher education and suspicious of bureaucratic institutions, even though they owed everything to them and could not imagine life outside them.

❧ ❧ ❧

The young New Critical foot soldiers Auden describes in "Under Which Lyre" weren't figments of his imagination. They did, in fact, pour into American colleges and universities after the war, thanks in large part to the Serviceman's Readjustment Act of 1944, more commonly known as the GI Bill. One place to find them in the historical record is on the rolls of the Kenyon School of English, launched by the poet-critic John Crowe Ransom in 1948. Two years after the Rockefeller little-magazine survey, which ultimately awarded his *Kenyon Review* the entirety of its allotted budget, Ransom received a three-year grant from the foundation to fund a summer program dedicated to training undergraduate teachers in criticism and critical theory. The same year, Blackmur was awarded a similar grant to establish the Christian Gauss Seminars in Criticism at Princeton. It would be institutionalized academic programs like these, rather than the work of little magazines, that would provide the way forward for the kind of discourse that modernist poet-critics had inaugurated.

It's no surprise that Ransom, in particular, appealed to university presidents and foundation officers. "If there was a single critical career whose personal trajectory perfectly coincided with the institutional fortunes of criticism," Gerald Graff writes in *Professing Literature*, "it was that of John Crowe Ransom."[2] Of all the poet-critics of the modernist era, it was Ransom who invested most deeply in the institution of the university, motivated not only by his commitment to the values of humanism but also by his awareness of a looming crisis within the professoriate. "I have an idea," he wrote to Allen Tate in 1937, apropos of his move from Vanderbilt to Kenyon and the creation of the *Kenyon Review*, "that we could really found criticism if we could get together on it. . . . The professors are in an awful dither trying to reform themselves and there's a big stroke possible for a small group that knows what it wants in giving them ideas and definitions and showing the way."[3] To a greater extent than any of his contemporaries, Ransom sought to found criticism, to give it a solid grounding in the practical and financial as well as the theoretical and intellectual sense. By the mid-1940s the high-minded ethical talk of principles that Eliot had inaugurated in the 1920s with essays like "The Function of Criticism," and that I. A. Richards had subsequently developed in *The Principles of Literary Criticism* and other theoretical texts, had now given way to the archaeological discourse of "foundation": the concern was not so much for an ethics or a methodology as it was the establishment of an institutional headquarters or home base.

Nor was Ransom's call for institutionalization expressed only in his private correspondence. "It is strange," he wrote in "Criticism, Inc.," first published in the *Virginia Quarterly Review* in the autumn of 1937 and reprinted the next year in his collection *The World's Body*, "but nobody seems to have told us what exactly is the proper business of criticism." Those currently writing criticism "have not been trained to criticism so much as they have simply undertaken a job for which no specific qualifications were required. It is far too likely that what they call criticism when they produce it is not the real thing."

So far, so Eliotic, especially when considered alongside Ransom's stated opinion that "probably the best critics of poetry we can now have are the poets." But he insists far more strongly than Eliot ever did on the limits of the practitioner's approach to criticism. "The artist himself . . . should know good art when he sees it," Ransom writes, "but his understanding is intuitive rather than dialectical—he cannot very well explain his theory of the thing." The need for theory, as much as the need for institutional financial support, undergirds Ransom's decisive call for a more rigorous, university-based culture of criticism:

> It is from the professors of literature, in this country the professors of English for the most part, that I should hope eventually for the erection of intelligent standards of criticism. It is their business. Criticism must become more scientific, or precise and systematic, and this means that it must be developed by the collective and sustained effort of learned persons—which means that its proper seat is in the universities. . . . Rather than occasional criticism by amateurs, I should think the whole enterprise might be seriously taken in hand by professionals. Perhaps I use a distasteful figure, but I have the idea that what we need is Criticism, Inc., or Criticism, Ltd.[4]

Already in 1937, Ransom sounds as if he were drafting a grant proposal, and indeed one can draw a direct line from "Criticism, Inc." to Ransom's 1948 proposal to the Rockefeller Foundation for what would become the Kenyon School of English. "Departments of English in American colleges and universities are not at all satisfied with the quota of first-rate students who elect English for their major study or for graduate work," the document begins. "The first-rate students who have made this election, in turn, often indicate their sense of the shortcomings of the English courses. This unhappy situation is of long standing, and has been evidenced most recently by expressions of discontent on the part of veterans returning to their studies." Linking the intellectual discontent that academic poet-critics like Ransom had long expressed to the specific situation of veterans was a savvy move, placing the New Criticism on the same side as the returning heroes of the war (and even drawing subconsciously, perhaps, on the association of philological scholarship with Germany). "It is our understanding that the English courses, as generally offered, do not have a proper regard either for the literary interest of their maturing students or for the possibilities of their subject," Ransom continued. "They devote themselves to a certain 'scholarship' which is admirable within limits, but beside the point when it goes too far. . . . We have then an instance of how a *means* may be pursued for its own sake without ever yielding the *end*."

In order to serve these dissatisfied graduate students, Ransom envisions a summer school populated by the most brilliant exemplars of the trend that he had already christened in his 1941 book *The New Criticism*. "The modern critics are publicly known by virtue of their writings," the proposal states. "But if these students could study personally under several of them as instructors, their own critical understanding could be instructed, and would be less private and uncertain. And since the students of English today are the teachers of English tomorrow, the teaching of English might be improved appreciably within a generation."

These terms—"improved appreciably within a generation"—would have been music to the ears of philanthropists who sought to cultivate lasting social change in ways that could be measured objectively. Moreover, where little magazines were, almost by definition, polemical and partisan, an institution like the Kenyon School of English was conceived from the start as gradualist and pluralistic. "The School of Criticism will not permit itself to be identified exclusively with any one critical 'position,'" Ransom emphasizes: the school's intention was not merely to advocate for immediate curricular or theoretical change within academic criticism, but to address root causes. Moreover, where the little magazine addressed itself to the elite, already educated reader, a project like the Kenyon School dedicated itself to the cultivation of a specific cadre of nonelite, undereducated readers, working with the raw material of the hundreds of young soldiers back from the war with a thirst for literature.[5]

Ransom and Kenyon College duly received a three-year grant of $40,000, funding a six-week summer course. Student expenses, including room and board, as well as tuition, came to roughly $250 for the term; each summer, about seventy-five students were enrolled, in addition to thirty-five auditors. Poet-critics were disproportionately well represented among the faculty; fellows in residence over the course of three summers included Ransom, William Empson, Allen Tate, Yvor Winters, Kenneth Burke, Cleanth Brooks, Robert Lowell, and Delmore Schwartz. Of the twenty-four courses offered over the course of the three years, fourteen were specifically poetry related. There were courses on individual authors (Milton, Keats, Wordsworth), as well as on broader topics like the English lyric and twentieth-century American poetry. Empson offered a class titled "The Key Word in the Long Poem" that would furnish material for his 1951 opus *The Structure of Complex Words*.

Looking over the class rosters for the Kenyon School of English's three consecutive summer sessions, one is struck by the relative diversity: roughly a quarter of the school's students were women, and Jewish names are common. Their number included future poets (Anthony Hecht) and theorists (Murray Krieger, who would go on to start the School of Criticism and Theory on a similar model in 1976). There is no way of telling how many of them had fought in the war, but one assumes that it was a sizable portion. These men and women—many of them anonymous, at least compared to the standards of their teachers—would make up the next generation of village explainers of modernism. The charismatic teachings of poet-critics like Ransom, Tate, Lowell, and Empson would be disseminated in lecture halls and seminar rooms across the nation. A feature article in the *Dallas Morning News* emphasized the probable long-term consequences of the undertaking: "The young men and women who this summer were the carefully chosen students of the Kenyon School of English will tomorrow, in all probability, be our most articulate teachers and critics." Describing the state of higher education in more apocalyptic terms than Ransom's proposal, the article attributed to "the Kenyonites" the view that the current method of graduate instruction "will not only destroy literature, but will undermine the broader critical sense of the vast reading public. It will drive us into a dullness which will prevent the development of valid literary and social judgments." The School of English thus took on some of the aspects of a civilizing mission: "If the Kenyon School succeeds in its objectives it will surely improve general literary taste. By training teachers who themselves are more alive to the exciting qualities of great literature and therefore able—even in required courses—to make prospective engineers, housewives, and businessmen more alive to those qualities, the school may develop more critical readers who will demand that the books all of us read be geared to more real and exacting standards."

For the first time, then, the essentially elitist critical agenda long advocated by modernist poet-critics like Eliot could appear as a populist educational project. "Next year there will be a hundred new students, and the year after, still another hundred," the newspaper enthused:

Not a large force, to be sure, when you consider the countless numbers in our giant industrial concerns. But through incisive criticism of their own work, as well as the works of others, the students at Kenyon are keeping alive a tradition and trying to arrive at values—literary and moral—for a world that has never before needed values so desperately. The people who cling to a conviction that the spoken and written word must be approached humanly and critically are perhaps the men and women in whom reside our most genuine hopes for tomorrow.

Whether we are professional students of literature or simply intelligent readers, all of us can in our quiet way help to carry those hopes.[6]

This was a new vision of modernist criticism, one completely compatible with the most respectable and patriotic American values—and thus partaking of some of the democratic rhetoric of the 1930s and 1940s, albeit depoliticized—but still intellectually serious and committed to critical standards. What would guarantee entry into the ranks of village explainers was not sensitivity or genius, as Eliot had imagined, or the strength of ethical or political commitment, as MacLeish had. Rather, it was education in the most formal sense: a credential in the art of criticism.

☙ ❧ ☙ ❧ ☙ ❧

It is here that the story of the modernist poet-critic begins to intersect with the rise of the creative writing program. "Creative and critical interests banded together to oppose the philological syndicate," D. G. Myers writes in *The Elephants Teach*, his history of creative writing. In his view, it was the infusion of energy and intellectual prestige that poet-critics like Ransom, Tate, Blackmur, Kenneth Burke, and Yvor Winters brought to the cause of criticism that finally allowed longtime exponents of academic criticism like Norman Foerster, J. E. Springarn, and R. S. Crane to triumph over the objections of skeptical philologists.[7] Graff endorses a similar theory when he claims that "many of the first critics to achieve a foothold in the university did so on the strength of their poetry rather than their criticism. It is worth pondering the probability that the critical movement would not have succeeded in the university had it not been tied to creative writing, from which it was soon to part company."[8]

As Graff suggests, the strategic alliance between creative writing and academic criticism was relatively short-lived; once each had gained sufficient prestige from the other to establish themselves as relatively autonomous disciplines, they soon retreated to their separate corners to cultivate a whole new narcissism of small differences. McGurl refers to "the sneering war between creative writers and scholars in the university, who upon the fading of the great poet-critics of the 1940s and 50s from the leading edge of literary scholarship came to seem divided by their shared object, literature, even as their offices were still often found side by side in the same hallways."[9] This transition would seem to call for a Weberian analysis of the profession, and in particular the rise of theory, in which the institution of academic literary criticism, founded on the charismatic authority of the modernist poet-critic, becomes bureaucratized and rationalized and has trouble legitimating itself in the absence of the original charismatic founders. After 1967, the charisma that had helped to establish criticism as an academic dis-

cipline has been largely channeled into the creative writing program, where, according to McGurl, "the literary artist [presents]
to students in the classroom . . . a charismatic model of *creative
being.*"[10]

At the same time, as McGurl also notes, the discipline of literary
study continues to address itself to theoretical issues arising out
of the practice of modernist poet-critics: "After World War II . . .
the modernist imperative to 'make it new' was institutionalized as
another form of original research sponsored by the booming,
science-oriented universities of the Cold War era."[11] Many of our
basic disciplinary assumptions—from the practice of close reading
to a theoretical concern for aesthetic autonomy to the shape of the
modern canon—are the result of this temporary alliance between
beleaguered poet-critics and beleaguered humanists against philologists and historians. The story of how the great modernist poet-
critics helped create the institutional conditions that made the New
Criticism, and subsequent developments in literary theory, possible
has a canonical status by now in literary studies. The problem with
this narrative is not that it is wrong; the problem is that it is partial,
and it reduces the manifold institutional commitments of poet-
critics like Eliot, Moore, Brown, Blackmur, and Ransom into a
"just-so story" to explain the evolution of a single academic discipline (ours). It is not at all surprising that so many literary scholars
have wanted to tell and retell this story, since it concludes with the
existence of literary studies as we currently know it: What child
isn't interested in hearing the story of her birth?

But modernist poet-critics, as I hope the foregoing has shown,
were trying to do more than found or reform an academic discipline, even if they ended up legitimizing two, and we should be
careful not to let the immense resonance that the *figure* of the poet-
critic has in academic life—for creative writers or, for that matter,
for critics—overdetermine our sense of those actual writers' own
commitments, priorities, and expectations, even when they now seem
utopian or unrealistic. As the political scientist Albert O. Hirschman
suggests regarding a different historical turning point—the expansion of capitalist civil society in the seventeenth and early eighteenth centuries—we may limit our understanding by attending to

the unexpected effects of what did happen at the expense of what was expected to happen but didn't: "On the one hand, there is no doubt that human actions and social decisions tend to have consequences that were entirely unintended at the outset. But, on the other hand, these actions and decisions are often taken because they are *earnestly and fully expected to have certain effects that then wholly fail to materialize.* . . . [T]he expectation of large, if unrealistic, benefits obviously serves to facilitate certain social decisions. Exploration and discovery of such expectations therefore help render social change more intelligible."[12]

I have tried to show that modernist poet-critics made deliberate social decisions about the relation of their work to postwar bureaucratic institutions, and that these decisions—alongside, of course, a multitude of other determining factors—led to significant change in the Anglo-American literary field. In the light of subsequent literary and institutional history, Ransom's governing idea—that the "proper seat" of literary criticism was in the universities—has gradually come to seem self-evident, but it was only one of many possible outcomes. From within the disciplinary matrix of the academic field that poet-critics have helped to initiate, the movement from poet-critics to New Criticism to theory may seem like inevitable and even intentional development, or it may seem like a tragic decline. In any case, by installing them as founding fathers and either blaming them for where we ended up or regretting that we lost sight of their mission, we risk projecting our present anxieties about our own precarious institutions onto our understanding of the critical decisions taken by these historical agents in their own moment. This is why it may help to return to the moment that these decisions were made: not because their effects were so significant, but because it can help us to reconstruct some of the assumptions and expectations modernist poet-critics had around the *idea* of institutionalization, and what contribution they felt they might be able to make to it. Today, as we contemplate new risks and new institutional arrangements, we have much to learn from them.

Notes

Introduction: Village Explainers

1. Gertrude Stein, *The Autobiography of Alice B. Toklas* (New York: Vintage, 1990), 200.

2. Wallace Stevens, *Letters of Wallace Stevens*, ed. Holly Stevens (Berkeley, CA: University of California Press, 1981), 362; William Carlos Williams, *Paterson* (New York: New Directions, 1992), 6; Archibald MacLeish, "Ars Poetica" in *Collected Poems, 1917–1982* (New York: Mariner, 1985), 106.

3. Mark McGurl, *The Program Era: Postwar Fiction and the Rise of Creative Writing* (Cambridge, MA: Harvard University Press, 2009), 48.

4. Although Adam Parkes claims that the term "poet-critic" did not appear in print before 1956, and it does seem to have come into general use only in the late 1950s, the word occasionally did crop up earlier. The *Oxford English Dictionary* lists an example without the hyphen from 1814, and George Saintsbury's chapter on Alexander Pope in his 1902 *History of Criticism and Literary Taste* contains the following sentence: "The poet-critic practically confesses the otiosity of the whole system by admitting that a lucky licence is a rule." Adam Parkes, "Poet-Critic," in *The Johns Hopkins Guide to Literary Theory and Criticism* (Baltimore, MD: Johns Hopkins University Press, 2005), 456; George Saintsbury, *History of Criticism and Literary Taste in Europe from the Earliest Texts to the Present*, vol. 2 (New York: Dodd, Mead, and Co., 1902), 456.

5. Thomas Piketty, *Capital in the Twenty-First Century*, trans. Arthur Goldhammer (Cambridge, MA: Harvard University Press, 2014), 135.

6. John Timberman Newcomb, *Would Poetry Disappear? American Verse and the Crisis of Modernity* (Columbus: Ohio State University Press, 2004), xxiii–xiv.

7. Lawrence Rainey, *Institutions of Modernism: Literary Elites and Public Culture* (New Haven, CT: Yale University Press, 1998), 3.

8. Ibid., 105.

9. See Eric Bennett, *Workshops of Empire: Stegner, Engle, and American Creative Writing during the Cold War* (Iowa City: University of Iowa Press, 2015); Greg Barnhisel, *Cold War Modernists: Art, Literature, and American Cultural Diplomacy* (New York: Columbia University Press, 2015); and Stephen

Schryer, *Fantasies of the New Class: Ideologies of Professionalism in Post–World War II American Fiction* (New York: Columbia University Press, 2011).

10. Langdon Hammer, *Hart Crane and Allen Tate: Janus-Faced Modernism* (Princeton, NJ: Princeton University Press, 1993), 27–28. Emphasis in original.

11. Luc Boltanski and Laurent Thévenot, *On Justification: Economies of Worth* (Princeton, NJ: Princeton University Press, 2006).

1

Imperfect Poet-Critics

1. Edmund Wilson, *Axel's Castle: A Study in the Imaginative Literature of 1870–1930* (New York: C. Scribner's Sons, 1932), 112.

2. René Wellek, "The Poet as Critic, the Critic as Poet, the Poet-Critic," in *The Poet as Critic*, ed. Frederick P. W. McDowell (Evanston, IL: Northwestern University Press, 1967), 273–274. Strangely, Wellek associates poet-critics (he names Eliot in particular later in the essay) with a reaction against the discourse of "pure" specialization: "Our time has reacted sharply against the 'pure' art, the 'pure' scholarship, and the 'pure' criticism of the early twentieth century. We don't want to be specialists, we want to be whole men; we want to reconcile the conscious and the unconscious, the life of the senses and the intellect. We want to have poet-critics. We can hope for them, but as the Devil's advocate, I can recommend beatification only in very rare cases, with veritable saints who have accomplished the miracle of reconciliation" (274).

3. This cursory sketch of the English critical field is adapted from John Gross, *The Rise and Fall of the Man of Letters: English Literary Life since 1800* (Chicago, IL: Ivan R. Dee, 1992). In large part Gross tells a story of the contestation of what had traditionally been journalistic territory by "Oxford and Cambridge products with smooth Oxford and Cambridge manners" such as Andrew Lang, George Saintsbury, and John Churton Collins (146). Those with political commitments included J. M. Robertson and C. F. G. Masterman on the liberal side and W. E. Henley, Charles Whibley, and George Wyndham on the Tory side; others, like G. K. Chesterton, had religious affiliations. A politically radical, but also aestheticist, tendency was represented by A. R. Orage and the *New Age*, which provided an early publication venue for Pound and Eliot. For an excellent study of Eliot's connections to literary journalism, see Jason Harding, *The "Criterion": Cultural Politics and Periodical Networks in Interwar Britain* (Oxford: Oxford University Press, 2002).

4. T. S. Eliot, "Professional, Or . . . ," in *The Complete Prose of T. S. Eliot: The Critical Edition: Apprentice Years, 1905–1918* (Baltimore, MD: Johns Hopkins University Press), 699.

5. T. S. Eliot, "Imperfect Critics," in *The Sacred Wood: Essays on Poetry and Criticism* (New York: Methuen, 1980), 46.

6. John Guillory puts this point very well when he suggests that "looking at the history of poetry from the point of view of the practicing poet . . . is the consistent feint of Eliot's critical prose." Guillory, *Cultural Capital: The*

Problem of Literary Canon Formation (Chicago, IL: University of Chicago Press, 1993), 147.

7. Eliot, "An American Critic," in *Complete Prose of T. S. Eliot*, 406.

8. Eliot, "The Perfect Critic," in *Sacred Wood*, 13.

9. Ibid., 5.

10. Ibid., 3.

11. Ibid., 6–7.

12. Ibid., 5.

13. Eliot, "Imperfect Critics," 17. When this essay was originally published in the *Athenaeum*, as "Swinburne and the Elizabethans," this sentence read: "Swinburne was writing not to establish a critical reputation, not to instruct a docile public, not like a grave condescending Arnold, but as a poet his notes upon poets whom he admired." The dig at Arnold was removed when the essay was reprinted in *The Sacred Wood*, in keeping with the "amends" that Eliot makes to him in the book's preface. Eliot, "Swinburne and the Elizabethans," *Athenaeum*, September 19, 1919.

14. Eliot, "Imperfect Critics," 19–20.

15. Ibid., 20–21.

16. Eliot, *Sacred Wood*, xi.

17. Ibid., xi–xii. See also Eliot's paraphrase from the lengthy section on Arnold in *The Use of Poetry and the Use of Criticism*:

> He is in some respects the most satisfactory man of letters of his age. . . . After the prophetic frenzies of the end of the eighteenth and the beginning of the nineteenth century, he seems to come to us saying: "This poetry is very fine, it is opulent and careless, it is sometimes profound, it is highly original; but you will never establish and maintain a tradition if you go on in this haphazard way. There are minor virtues which have flourished better at other times and in other countries: these you must give heed to, these you must apply, in your poetry, in your prose, in your conversation and your way of living; else you condemn yourselves to enjoy only fitful and transient bursts of literary brilliance, and you will never, as a people, a nation, a race, have a fully formed tradition and personality."

T. S. Eliot, *The Use of Poetry and the Use of Criticism: Studies in the Relation of Criticism to Poetry in England* (Cambridge, MA: Harvard University Press, 1986), 96–97.

18. Eliot, *Sacred Wood*, xii.

19. Ibid., xi.

20. Ibid., xiii.

21. Eliot, "A Brief Treatise on the Criticism of Poetry," in *The Complete Prose of T. S. Eliot: The Critical Edition*, vol. 2, *The Perfect Critic, 1919–1926*, ed. Anthony Cuda and Ronald Schuchard (Baltimore, MD: Johns Hopkins University Press, 2014), 207.

22. Eliot, *Sacred Wood*, xiv.

23. Eliot, "Gerontion" in *The Waste Land and Other Writings* (New York: Modern Library, 2001), 22–24.

2

Picking and Choosing

1. For a thorough account and analysis of this correspondence, see Lois Bar-Yaccov, "The Odd Couple: The Correspondence between Marianne Moore and Ezra Pound, 1918–1939," *Twentieth Century Literature* 34, no. 4 (Winter 1988): 507–527.

2. Marianne Moore, *The Selected Letters of Marianne Moore*, ed. Bonnie Costello, Celeste Goodridge, and Cristanne Miller (New York: Penguin, 1998), 122–123.

3. The first sentence is taken from Moore's 1921 review of *Kora in Hell* by William Carlos Williams (Patricia C. Willis, ed., *The Complete Prose of Marianne Moore* [New York: Viking, 1986], 56). The second is from "The Past Is the Present," a poem originally published in 1917 in Moore, *Becoming Marianne Moore: The Early Poems, 1907–1924*, ed. Robin Schulze (Berkeley: University of California Press, 2002), 74.

4. Mark Van Doren, "Women of Wit," in *The Critical Response to Marianne Moore*, ed. Elizabeth Gregory (Westport, CT: Prager, 2003), 33. Emphasis added.

5. Louis Untermeyer, "Poetry or Wit?," in *Critical Response to Marianne Moore*, 47. Emphasis added.

6. Although, demonstrating that disapproval of Moore's "critical" poetics was not an exclusively male prejudice, Harriet Monroe, in her 1922 "Symposium on Marianne Moore," published in *Poetry*, wrote that Moore's "mood yields prose oftener than poetry. . . . No amount of line-patterning can make anything but statement and argument out of many of the entries in this book.'" Harriet Monroe, "Symposium on Marianne Moore" in *Critical Response to Marianne Moore*, 38.

7. Untermeyer, "Poetry or Wit?," 49.

8. As Rachel Blau DuPlessis has observed, Moore was often paired in this connection with her contemporary Mina Loy, notably by Pound in a 1917 review that tagged both women as practitioners of "logopoeia" (defined as "a dance of the intelligence among words and ideas"). In contrast to the more conventionally feminine lyric writing that DuPlessis terms "poesy," "a writer of logopoeia produces a poetry of ideas and wordplay, intellectual allusions made in poetry, dissenting resistant analytics, discursive gear stripping." DuPlessis goes on to make a convincing argument for logopoeia as grounded in "a feminist analysis of the gender assumptions of lyric" arising from "poetry written from the subject position of the New Woman": "The desire not for beauty but for diagnosis—a diagnosis that undercuts poesy—is most imperiously a diagnosis of poetry's own gender assumptions." Rachel Blau DuPlessis, "Corpses of Poesy: Some Modern Poets and Some Gender Ideologies of Lyric," in *Feminist Measures: Soundings in Poetry and Theory*, ed. Cristanne Miller and Lynn Keller (Ann Arbor: University of Michigan Press, 1994), 77.

9. Quoted in Taffy Martin, *Marianne Moore, Subversive Modernist* (Austin: University of Texas Press, 2012), 33.

10. Gorham B. Munson, *Destinations: A Canvass of American Literature since 1900* (New York: J. H. Sears, 1928), 99–100. Emphasis in original.

11. Suzanne Churchill, "Making Space for *Others*: A History of a Modernist Little Magazine," *Journal of Modern Literature* 22, no. 1 (Fall 1998): 48.

12. Moore, *Becoming Marianne Moore*, 77–78.

13. Moore's first poem explicitly on the subject of aesthetic judgment was itself an aesthetic breakthrough, as Linda Leavell has noted: it marked the appearance of "the first fully realised Moore stanza." Linda Leavell, *Prismatic Color: Marianne Moore and the Visual Arts* (Baton Rouge: Louisiana State University Press, 1995), 72. In other words, according to Leavell's sensitive reading, the theme of the poem echoes its form: "'Unconscious fastidiousness' . . . describes the paradoxical nature of Moore's stanza that she was just perfecting at the time she wrote 'Critics and Connoisseurs'" (167). This is important because it links Moore herself, qua poet, to the "critics and connoisseurs" she discusses, a point that has not been evident to Moore scholars. In *The Poetry of Engagement*, for instance, Grace Schulman reads the poem as an outright allegorical attack on shallow sophistication: "As in the fable, there is a moral: 'ambition without understanding' is futile. An ant in the speaker's memory, like the unenlightened swan, is unable to learn from past experience and carries heavy burdens though it knows the procedure is useless. . . . [T]he swan and ant . . . embody the condition of being the dense pretenders of the title." Grace Schulman, *Marianne Moore: The Poetry of Engagement* (Urbana: University of Illinois Press, 1986), 37, 53. This excessively negative reading of the poem seems unwarranted, however, when one considers the degree of appreciation that the speaker has for the fastidiousness (both conscious and unconscious) of the swan and the ant, and her admission that "there is a great amount of poetry" in their movements. Leavell is closer to the mark when she claims that "most critics do themselves an injustice when they give it [the poem's opening lines] the negative interpretation, 'There is *no* poetry in the *conscious* fastidiousness of critics and connoisseurs.' . . . [W]hen she describes the fastidiousness of the swan and ant in 'Critics and Connoisseurs,' she also speaks with admiration, qualified only by the fact that she likes unconscious fastidiousness better" (165).

14. For a useful overview of the transfer of editorial power at the *Dial* during this period, see Nicholas Joost, *Scofield Thayer and "The Dial": An Illustrated History* (Carbondale: Southern Illinois University Press, 1964), 3–23.

15. Ibid., 112.

16. "Announcement," *The Dial* 78 (June 1925), 532.

17. Moore, *Becoming Marianne Moore*, 97–98.

18. After 1925, when Moore took over active management of the *Dial*, Thayer's direct sphere of influence was circumscribed to visual art alone. By contrast, according to Nicholas Joost, "Moore's relation to the pictures in *The Dial* [after becoming editor] continued to be one of appreciation rather than of industrious engagement with their selection. Pictures continued to be bought

by Scofield Thayer and Dr. Watson—usually by Scofield Thayer" (*Scofield Thayer*, 97–98). For an instructive discussion of the place of visual art in the *Dial*, see ibid., 46–52.

19. Moore, *Becoming Marianne Moore*, 101.

20. Linda Leavell has argued that Thayer took a romantic interest in Moore, even to the point of proposing marriage, a conjecture on which my argument does not depend, but one that, if true, makes her psychological investment in him still more fascinating. See Leavell, "Frightening Disinterestedness: The Personal Circumstances of Marianne Moore's 'Marriage,'" *Journal of Modern Literature* 31, no. 1 (Fall 2007): 64–79. I would like to draw particular attention to a passage Leavell quotes from a letter Moore wrote to her brother Warner in 1920, describing an early encounter with Thayer: "Scofield has a gorgeous library . . . about 3 walls full of light calf bindings or blue bindings, a grate full of ashes a foot deep and a yellow desk like yours, not quite so large. . . . He showed me his art treasures (upon request), a large black marble, nude, some Beardsley pen drawings—a 'cubist painting' and some drawings of dancers" (Moore, *Selected Letters*, 135, quoted by Leavell, 67). Already by 1920, a year before the original version of "When I Buy Pictures" was published, a specific interest in Thayer's "art treasures" accompanied her general impressions of his wealth and social prestige.

3

Student Bodies

1. I. A. Richards, "On TSE: Notes for a Talk at the Institute of Contemporary Arts, London, June 29, 1965," in *T. S. Eliot: The Man and His Work*, ed. Allen Tate (New York: Delacorte, 1966), 2–3.

2. Louis Menand, *Discovering Modernism: T. S. Eliot and His Context* (New York: Oxford University Press, 2007), 154.

3. F. W. Bateson, "T.S. Eliot: 'Impersonality Fifty Years After,'" quoted in Menand, *Discovering Modernism*, 154.

4. James Reeves, "Cambridge Twenty Years Ago," in *T. S. Eliot: A Symposium*, ed. Tambimuttu and Richard March (London: Frank & Cass, 1965), 38.

5. Ibid., 39.

6. We should note that the vogue for Eliot at Cambridge was, as James Reeves emphasizes, mostly among the undergraduates rather than the professors: "Those who played the part of sidesmen were not, it should perhaps be said, my tutors but my fellow-undergraduates. Eliot was not at this time 'officially' recognized." He elaborates: "The attitude of the English school varied according to the temperament of the lecturers; the more rebellious were enthusiastic, the more conventional loudly and derisively hostile. The 'centre' were temperately and critically sympathetic towards what they recognized as an important new influence, even though it was hailed with undiscriminating adulation by intellectual undergraduates." Ibid., 38.

7. Ibid., 35.

8. Kathleen Raine, "The Poet of Our Time," in *T. S. Eliot: A Symposium*, 78.

9. *The Letters of T. S. Eliot*, vol. 1, *1898–1922*, ed. Valerie Eliot (New York: Harcourt Brace Jovanovich, 1988), 74–75.

10. Stephen Spender recalls, for example, that his first meeting with Eliot "must have been at University College, Oxford, when he addressed an undergraduate club, the Martlets, on Wednesday, May 16, 1928. . . . Eliot attended the meeting of the Martlets, on the condition that he should not give an address, but would answer questions only." Stephen Spender, "Remembering Eliot," in Tate, *T. S. Eliot: The Man and His Work*, 38. As for Eliot's All Souls fellowship, his biographer Peter Ackroyd suggests that his application was rejected on the basis of his poetic reputation: "After [the fellows] had seen his latest volume of poetry, they decided he was not quite what they were looking for: *Poems 1909–1925* was too modern, too iconoclastic." Peter Ackroyd, *T. S. Eliot: A Life* (New York: Simon and Schuster, 1984), 157.

11. Spender, "Remembering Eliot," 57.

12. Ibid., 43–44.

13. Ibid., 48.

14. W. H. Auden, *The Complete Works of W. H. Auden: Prose*, vol. 1, *1926–1938* (Princeton, NJ: Princeton University Press, 1997), 25.

15. Auden, "Private Pleasure," in *The Complete Works*, 28.

16. Auden, "The Liberal Fascist (Honour)," in *The Complete Works*, 59.

17. Stephen Burt, *The Forms of Youth: Twentieth-Century Poetry and Adolescence* (New York: Columbia University Press, 2007), 51.

18. Christopher Isherwood, *Lions and Shadows: An Education in the Twenties* (Minneapolis: University of Minnesota Press, 2000), 184.

19. Matters are made still more complex by the fact that "Address for a Prize-Day" is also a parody of one of Auden's acknowledged literary sources for *The Orators*: D. H. Lawrence's *Fantasia of the Unconscious*. Lawrence's 1922 text, with its clipped sentences, direct address, macho camp, and aggressively rhetorical questions, exerted an immense influence on the young Auden. It is possible, then, that "Address for a Prize-Day" was in part an attempt to exorcise that influence by lampooning the oratorical, even oracular, tendencies inherent in Lawrentian modernism.

20. W. H. Auden, *The English Auden: Poems, Essays, and Dramatic Writings, 1927–1939*, ed. Edward Mendelson (London: Faber and Faber, 1988), 61.

21. Ibid., 61–62.

22. Ibid., 64.

23. Edward Mendelson, *Early Auden* (New York: Farrar, Straus & Giroux, 2000), 94.

24. W. H. Auden, foreword to *The Orators* (London: Faber and Faber, 1966), 7.

25. Richard Davenport-Hines, introduction to "School Writings," in *"The Language of Learning and the Language of Love": Uncollected Writing, New Interpretations*, ed. Katharine Bucknell and Nicholas Jenkins (Oxford: Oxford University Press, 1994), 2.

26. Ibid., 1.

27. Auden, *English Auden*, 96.

28. Ibid., 98. "Ghillie" or "gillie" is a Scottish dialect term that refers to a man or a boy who acts as an attendant on a fishing or hunting expedition,

primarily in Scotland in the Highlands or on a river such as the Spey River. In origin it referred especially to someone who attended on his employer or guests. George Orwell, in his scathing public school memoir "Such, Such Were the Joys," writes that "at the beginning and end of the term . . . there was naively snobbish chatter about Switzerland, and Scotland with its ghillies and grouse moors, and 'my uncle's yacht,' and 'our place in the country,' and 'my pony' and 'my pater's touring car.'" George Orwell, *Facing Unpleasant Facts* (New York: Mariner, 2008), 279.

29. Karl Marx, *Critique of Hegel's "Philosophy of Right,"* trans. Annette Jolin and Joseph O'Malley (Cambridge: Cambridge University Press, 1978), 131.

30. Stan Smith, "The Dating of Auden's 'Who Will Endure' and the Politics of 1931," *Review of English Studies*, n.s., 41, no. 163 (August 1990): 362.

31. Marx, *Critique*, 132.

32. Ibid., 133.

33. Ibid., 133–134.

34. Auden, *English Auden*, 98.

4

Interrupting the Muse

1. The deterioration of MacLeish's reputation after the 1940s and even more after his death in 1982 is remarkable, given how seriously he was taken in his own time. John Timberman Newcomb lumps MacLeish's "decanonization" together with that of other progressive poets of the 1930s like Carl Sandburg and Muriel Rukeyser, making an argument similar to that of Cary Nelson's *Repression and Recovery*. See John Timberman Newcomb, "Archibald MacLeish and the Poetics of Public Speech: A Critique of High Modernism" in *The Journal of the Midwest Modern Language Association*, 23 no. 1 (Spring 1990): 9. Greg Barnhisel, too, views MacLeish's demotion as primarily an ideological matter: "His earnest, vocally pro-American liberalism didn't fit with modernism's political profile; his lines began to look less like Eliot's or Pound's and more like those of out-of-favor poets such as Carl Sandburg and Vachel Lindsay." Barnhisel, *Cold War Modernists: Art, Literature, and American Cultural Diplomacy* (New York: Columbia University Press, 2015), 37–38.

A more detailed and more convincing account of the phenomenon is given by Michael Augspurger, who notes that MacLeish was unpopular with many of his contemporaries even in the 1930s. Edmund Wilson, for instance, published a "scathing" parody called "The Omelet of A. MacLeish" in the *New Yorker* in 1939, and both his poetry and his politics were frequently attacked in the pages of *Partisan Review*. Given how influential both Wilson and *Partisan Review* were on literary taste both inside and outside the academy from the 1940s onward, it's not surprising that MacLeish has fallen—more or less permanently, it seems—out of fashion. See Michael Augspurger, "Archibald MacLeish and Professional Leadership," *College Literature* 36, no. 4 (Fall 2009): 1–3, 20–22.

2. *Letters of Archibald MacLeish: 1907–1982*, ed. R. H. Winnick (New York: Houghton Mifflin, 1983), 291.

3. Ibid., 299.

4. Ibid., 300.

5. Ibid., 294.

6. Archibald MacLeish, "Invocation to the Social Muse," in *Collected Poems, 1917–1982* (New York: Mariner, 1985), 295–297.

7. Archibald MacLeish, *A Time to Speak: The Selected Prose of Archibald MacLeish* (New York: Houghton Mifflin, 1940), 14.

8. Ibid., 103.

9. Ibid., 104.

10. Ibid., 115. Emphasis in original.

11. Ibid., 112.

12. Mark Greif, *The Age of the Crisis of Man: Thought and Fiction in America, 1933–1973* (Princeton, NJ: Princeton University Press), 24. Emphasis in original.

13. MacLeish, *A Time to Speak*, 121.

14. Ira Katznelson, *Fear Itself: The New Deal and the Origins of Our Time* (New York: Liveright, 2013).

15. Augspurger, "Archibald MacLeish and Professional Leadership," 3.

16. MacLeish, *Time to Speak*, 77–78.

17. Newcomb, *Would Poetry Disappear?*, passim.

18. MacLeish, *Time to Speak*, 24.

19. Archibald MacLeish, "America Was Promises," in *Collected Poems*, 331.

20. Barnhisel, *Cold War Modernists*, 2–3.

21. Michael Hiltzik, *The New Deal: A Modern History* (New York: Free Press, 2011), 293.

22. Michael Szalay, *New Deal Modernism: American Literature and the Invention of the Welfare State* (Durham, NC: Duke University Press, 2000), 14.

23. Hiltzik, *New Deal*, 286.

24. For an excellent discussion of the bureaucratic context of the FWP and its contribution to literary and cultural diversity in the United States, see Wendy Griswold, *American Guides: The Federal Writers' Project and the Casting of American Culture* (Chicago: University of Chicago Press, 2016).

25. Charles S. Johnson, letter to Sterling A. Brown, June 19, 1928, from the Sterling A. Brown Collection at the Moorland-Springarn Research Center (MSRC), Howard University, Washington, DC. Reprinted by permission of Elizabeth A. Dennis. Johnson returns to the trope of "superiority" and "advantage" in his letter of May 25, 1932: "I told my class that you were drawing a new pattern, . . . You have a superior advantage, from the point of view of the classical tradition, to most of the writers today . . . and in turning to the medium of the folk Negro for expression, it is the supreme mark of the conscious Negro artist." Johnson, letter to Brown, May 25, 1932, MSRC.

26. Lawrence P. Jackson, *The Indignant Generation: A Narrative History of African American Writers and Critics, 1934–1960* (Princeton, NJ: Princeton University Press, 2011), 37.

27. Sterling A. Brown, "Our Literary Audience," in *A Son's Return: Selected Essays of Sterling A. Brown*, ed. Mark Sanders (Boston: Northeastern University Press, 1996), 144–148. Emphasis in original.

28. Langston Hughes, "The Negro Artist and the Racial Mountain," in *The Collected Works of Langston Hughes, Vol. 9: Essays on Art, Race, Politics, and World Affairs*, ed. Christopher C. DeSantis (Columbia: University of Missouri Press, 2002), 32.

29. Charles H. Rowell, "'Let Me Be with Ole Jazzbo': An Interview with Sterling A. Brown," *Callaloo* 14, no. 4 (Autumn 1991): 812–813.

30. Brent Edwards, "The Seemingly Eclipsed Window of Form: James Weldon Johnson's Prefaces," in *The Jazz Cadence of American Culture*, ed. Robert G. O'Meally (New York: Columbia University Press, 1998), 585. Emphasis in original.

31. Sterling A. Brown, *The Collected Poems of Sterling A. Brown*, ed. Michael S. Harper (Evanston, IL: TriQuarterly Books/Northwestern University Press, 2000), 26–30.

32. Brown, "Strong Men," in *Collected Poems*, 56.

33. Sterling A. Brown, "Negro Character as Seen by White Authors," in *Son's Return*, 182.

34. Todd Carmody, "Sterling Brown and the Dialect of New Deal Optimism," *Callaloo* 33, no. 3 (2010): 821.

35. Brown, letter to Henry Alsberg, April 14, 1936, MSRC. Brown letters copyright by Sterling A. Brown. Reprinted by permission of Elizabeth A. Dennis.

36. Brown, letter to Charles S. Johnson, May 27, 1936, MSRC.

37. Brown, letter to Charles S. Johnson, August 5, 1936, MSRC.

38. Brown, letter to Charles Jones, January 14, 1939, MSRC.

39. Brown, letter to T. Arnold Hill, August 11, 1939, MSRC.

40. Carmody, "Sterling Brown and the Dialect of New Deal Optimism," 820.

41. Brown, letter to J. H. Harmon Jr., October 27, 1936, MSRC.

42. Ulysses P. Lee, letter to Brown, June 30, 1936, MSRC.

43. Carmody, "Sterling Brown and the Dialect of New Deal Optimism," 825.

44. Brown, letter to Roscoe Lewis, September 4, 1936, MSRC.

45. Szalay, *New Deal Modernism*, 6, 28.

46. Roscoe Lewis, letter to Brown, n.d. [1937/1938], MSRC.

47. Brown, letter to Roscoe Lewis, n.d. [1937/1938], MSRC.

48. Roscoe Lewis, letter to Brown, March 8, 1939, MSRC.

49. Brown, letter to Roscoe Lewis, September 11, 1939, MSRC.

50. Brown, letter to Roscoe Lewis, April 21, 1939, MSRC.

51. Roscoe Lewis, letter to Brown, September 7, 1937, MSRC.

52. Brown, letter to Roscoe Lewis, September 11, 1939, MSRC. "Jump back, honey, jump back" is a refrain from "A Negro Love Song" by Paul Laurence Dunbar.

53. Brown, letter to Roscoe Lewis, April 6, 1939, MSRC.

54. Brown, *Son's Return*, 87.

5

The Foundations of Criticism

1. R. P. Blackmur, "The Economy of the American Writer: Preliminary Notes," *Sewanee Review* 53, no. 12 (Spring 1945): 175.

2. Ibid., 179, 184.

3. Ibid., 176.

4. Ibid.

5. Ibid., 181.

6. Michael Szalay, *New Deal Modernism: American Literature and the Invention of the Welfare State* (Durham: Duke University Press, 2000).

7. Blackmur, "Economy of the American Writer," 178.

8. Ibid., 185.

9. Ibid.

10. Olivier Zunz, *Philanthropy in America: A History* (Princeton, NJ: Princeton University Press), 4.

11. Ibid., 22, 169.

12. Ibid., 4, 21.

13. Ibid., 155.

14. Mark Dowie, *American Foundations: An Investigative History* (Cambridge, MA: MIT Press, 2001), x.

15. Zunz, *Philanthropy in America*, 25–26.

16. My information on the Rockefeller Foundation's history is drawn chiefly from Waldemar A. Nielsen, *The Big Foundations* (New York: Columbia University Press, 1972); Abraham Flexner, *Funds and Foundations: Their Policies Past and Present* (New York: Harper and Brothers, 1952); and William J. Buxton, ed., *Patronizing the Public: American Philanthropy's Transformation of Culture, Communication, and the Humanities* (Lanham, MD: Lexington Books, 2009). "The Humanities Division lacked the prestige of the other major Rockefeller Divisions," Buxton writes. "Its lower status was reflected in its modest budget [$750,000 per year], which made it difficult for it to have an impact comparable with that of the better-funded Divisions" (Buxton, "John Marshall and the Humanities in Europe," in Buxton, *Patronizing the Public*, 133–134). The "neglect of the humanities" was rued by one-time General Education Board director Abraham Flexner: "The thoughtful reader of these pages must have been struck by the crying inadequacy of the funds devoted to humanistic studies—to languages, literature, art, archaeology, philosophy, music, history.... Can one imagine the triumphant shout of approval that would greet such action on the part of a foundation in position to furnish the means for such a development?" Flexner, *Funds and Foundations*, 129–130.

17. My emphasis on extra-academic projects, particularly in communications, follows Buxton's. Nielsen is less impressed by Stevens's and Marshall's attempts to expand the humanities program beyond the academy: "The Division of the Arts and Humanities under David H. Stevens inherited a rather academic tradition from its predecessor in the GEB and dutifully perpetuated it. The program continued to emphasize archeology, scholarly research in ancient cultures, and classical humanistic research. The general effect, as various observers, including the director of the foundation's program himself, remarked, was to buttress 'scholasticism and antiquarianism in our universities.'" Nielsen, *Big Foundations*, 59–60.

18. For an excellent overview and analysis of these Rockefeller projects, see "Mobilizing for the War on Words: The Rockefeller Foundation, Communi-

cation Scholars, and the State" in Brett Gary, *The Nervous Liberals: Propaganda Anxieties from World War I to the Cold War* (New York: Columbia University Press, 1999).

19. John Marshall, letter to David H. Stevens, September 18, 1946, box 7, folder 17, R. P. Blackmur Papers (Co227) (RPBP), Manuscripts Division Department of Rare Books and Special Collections, Princeton University Library, Princeton, NJ.

20. Blackmur, undated letter to various respondents, box 7, folder 17, RPBP.

21. Edmund Wilson, letter to Blackmur, November 6, 1946, box 9, folder 12, RPBP; Eric Bentley, letter to Blackmur, November 10, 1946, box 1, folder 10, RPBP.

22. Alfred Kazin, letter to Blackmur, November 1, 1946, box 5, folder 3, RPBP; F. O. Matthiessen, letter to Blackmur, November 10, [1946], box 5, folder 11, RPBP; Robert Penn Warren, letter to Blackmur, November 11, 1946, box 9, folder 5, RPBP; Kenneth Burke, letter to Blackmur, November 18, 1946, box 2, folder 9, RPBP.

23. Marianne Moore, letter to Blackmur, November 2, 1946, box 6, folder 8, RPBP.

24. Randall Jarrell, letter to Blackmur, ca. 1946, box 4, folder 17, RPBP.

25. William Carlos Williams, letter to Blackmur, November 11, 1946, box 9, folder 11, RPBP.

26. W. H. Auden, letter to Blackmur, December 11, 1946, box 1, folder 9, RPBP.

27. Matthiessen, letter to Blackmur.

28. Auden, letter to Blackmur.

29. Louise Bogan, letter to Blackmur, August 21, 1946, box 1, folder 11, RPBP.

30. Wallace Stevens, letter to Blackmur, November 12, 1946, box 8, folder 9, RPBP.

31. Stevens wrote to Blackmur: "Why not try to [enlist] support for the contributors instead of the magazines. . . . You would be getting more of what you want for your money and you would still be leaving it necessary for the magazines themselves to show their good faith, not to speak of many things just as fundamental, in their struggle for existence." From this proposal, it should be clear that what bothered Stevens was not remuneration for writers per se—he would have been fine with the patronage system of an earlier era, for instance—but economic self-interest as a motive force guiding the production of literary work. Funding writers directly, rather than little magazines, would eliminate the need for such rational calculation and allow them to produce as they pleased (although in practice, the choice of which writers to support would still be a matter of rationalization and justification).

32. Kenneth E. Boulding, "A Theory of Philanthropy," in *Collected Papers*, ed. Fred R. Glahe (Boulder: Colorado University Associated Press, 1971), 2:238.

33. Ibid., 2:241.

34. Williams, letter to Blackmur.

Conclusion: With the Program

1. Auden, "Under Which Lyre," in *Collected Poems* (New York: Vintage, 1991), 333–339.

2. Gerald Graff, *Professing Literature: An Institutional History* (Chicago, IL: University of Chicago Press, 1987), 155.

3. Quoted in ibid., 157.

4. John Crowe Ransom, "Criticism, Inc.," in *The World's Body* (New York: Scribner's, 1938), 328–329.

5. "The Kenyon School of Criticism: A Plan for an Educational Project in the Humanities," Kenyon School of English, Box 1B, Greenslade Special Collections and Archives, Kenyon College. Emphasis in original.

6. David Zesmer, "Experiment at Kenyon in 'New Criticism,'" *Dallas Morning News*, September 5, 1948. Kenyon School of English, Box 1H, Greenslade Special Collections and Archives, Kenyon College.

7. D.G. Myers, *The Elephants Teach: Creative Writing Since 1880* (Chicago, IL: University of Chicago Press, 1996), 128–131.

8. Graff, *Professing Literature*, 153.

9. Mark McGurl, *The Program Era: Postwar Fiction and the Rise of Creative Writing* (Cambridge, MA: Harvard University Press, 2009), 8–9.

10. Ibid., 36.

11. Ibid., 4.

12. Albert O. Hirschman, *The Passions and the Interests: Political Arguments for Capitalism Before its Triumph* (Princeton, NJ: Princeton University Press, 1977), 130–131. Emphasis in original.

Acknowledgments

I N THE COURSE of producing this book, I've incurred an immense number of debts. I am enormously fortunate to have a generous and tireless mentor in Susan Stewart, a brilliant poet-critic and a model for the balance of scholarly rigor and intellectual creativity that I continue to strive for in my own work. I am also grateful for the advice, direction, and support of Jeremy Braddock, James Longenbach, Meredith Martin, and Michael Wood, all of whom helped to shape the project at a crucial early stage.

At Princeton University, I benefited greatly from conversations with Jason Baskin, Adrienne Brown, John Bugg, Jeff Dolven, William Evans, Jonathan Foltz, Diana Fuss, Rachel Galvin, Michael Johnduff, Greg Londe, Joseph Moshenska, Jeff Nunokawa, Sonya Posmentier, Ethel Rackin, Lindsay Reckson, James Richardson, David Russell, Keri Walsh, and Dora Zhang. In subsequent years many scholars and friends have read portions of the manuscript at various stages and provided help, advice, and encouragement. I would like to thank Greg Barnhisel, C. D. Blanton, Sarah Brouillette, Franklin Bruno, Stephen Burt, Michael Clune, Kevin Dettmar, Boris Dralyuk, Merve Emre, James English, John Farrell, Rachel Galvin, Andrew Goldstone, Mark Greif, Andy Hines, Claire Jarvis, Lee Konstantinou, Aaron Kunin, Mark McGurl, Richard Jean So, Juliana Spahr, Robert Von Hallberg, Jeffrey Williams, and Ben Wurgaft.

I have been lucky to find a welcoming and diverse intellectual community in Los Angeles. Brian Kim Stefans graciously invited me to share my research in progress with his Modernist Experimental

Literature and Text working group at UCLA. The Southern California Americanist Group, hosted by the Huntington Library in Pasadena, has provided an invaluable forum for sharing work in progress and trying out ideas; I'd like to thank Michelle Chihara, Aaron DeRosa, Bert Emerson, Thomas Koenigs, Lisa Mendelman, Sarah Mesle, Siobhan Phillips, Christian Reed, and everyone else who participated in those discussions. I would also like to thank my colleagues at Claremont McKenna College and at the *Los Angeles Review of Books*, particularly Tom Lutz, who has provided me with an opportunity to see how literary institutions function up close.

Thanks to Lindsay Waters, my editor at Harvard University Press, for his early enthusiasm for my work, and to Amanda Peery, Joy Deng, Stephanie Vyce, Michael Higgins, and everyone else at Harvard for their help bringing this project to fruition.

Versions of Chapters 2 and 5 are informed by my earlier articles in *English Literary History* and *Critical Inquiry;* I thank the editors of those journals for their role in improving the texts and guiding me toward new questions and insights. A version of Chapter 3 further examines topics initially deliberated in my contribution to the anthology *Auden at Work*, edited by Bonnie Costello and Rachel Galvin; thanks to them for their guidance and for inviting me to contribute. I would also like to thank the Department of Rare Books and Special Collections at Princeton University Library in Princeton, the Moorland-Springarn Research Collection at Howard University in Washington, D.C., and the Greenslade Special Collections and Archives at Kenyon College in Gambier, Ohio, for permission to quote from archival materials.

To my father, Jeffrey Kindley, I owe my interests in poetry and criticism; to my mother, Louise Kindley, my interests in institutions and social life. This book in some ways reflects a blend of their sensibilities and priorities. It could not have been completed without their support. My mother-in-law, Margaret Ryan, and my father-in-law, Steven Lerner, also have my gratitude and my affection. And I am thankful every day for my brilliant and loving wife, Emily Ryan Lerner, and for our daughter, Agnes.

Index